Picture Framing
·A MANUAL OF TECHNIQUES·
David Scholes

Picture Framing
·A MANUAL OF TECHNIQUES·

David Scholes

The Crowood Press

First published in 1995 by
The Crowood Press Ltd
Ramsbury, Marlborough
Wiltshire SN8 2HR

British Library Cataloguing in Publication Data

A catalogue record for this book is available from the British Library.

ISBN 1 85223 879 8

Picture Credits
Photographs by David Scholes
Line-drawings by Anthony Phillips-Smith

Typeset by Dorwyn Ltd, Rowlands Castle, Hants
Printed and bound by The Bath Press

Contents

	Acknowledgements	6
	Introduction	7
1	Tools and Materials	9
2	Making a Frame	17
3	Glass and Glass Cutting	34
4	Mounts and Mount Cutting	46
5	Mount Decoration	70
6	Mouldings	88
7	Framing Needlework and Embroidery	103
8	Framing Pieces with Depth	114
9	Final Assembly and Finishing	120
	Index	127

Acknowledgements

My thanks to Black and Decker for supplying a BD 564 drill and a BD780E router; to Daler-Rowney for supplying the technical data of their Studland mountboard, conservation and museum board, along with a range of their coloured and pearlescent inks, their oval and circle cutter, and a variety of hand-held and straight-line cutters; to Fiddes and Son for their wood stain, sealer and polishes; to Liberon Waxes Ltd for their range of frame fillers, gilt-filler sticks, gilt pencils, gilt varnish, Fontenay base and ready-made gesso; and to Mark Soloman of Framers Equipment. My thanks also go to Graham Clarke for permission to use his etchings Albert All, Johnny Garlic Sausage and Keep your Saxon in the section on cutting arch-top mounts, to Ian Cox of Rozen Furniture for his generous supply of specialist wood used for machining, and to my friends Jeremy Williams for his practical guidance and Tony Phillips-Smith for his excellent illustrations. Finally to my wife Sue for her practical help and encouragement during the many times of mental block encountered throughout this project.

Introduction

When you hang the first picture you have mounted and framed yourself it will be with a great feeling of pride and accomplishment. You will have used several skills, both artistic and practical, in the process of choosing and mitring the moulding and cutting the mount. Basic carpentry and cutting skills are of course necessary, but the choice of moulding and mount is purely a question of individual preference since everyone has his own ideas and feelings about pictures and frames. There are no hard and fast rules; my thoughts are that if it pleases you it is a success.

Why do we put a picture in a frame? For protection? Yes. To make it look finished? Yes. To improve the picture? No: a frame – no matter how decorative or expensive – will never make a poor picture good; it may take your attention temporarily away from its shortcomings but it will never overcome them. A frame should complement the subject, and enhance it, not compete with it. For example, a photograph of a child dressed in bright modern clothing would look out of place in a very ornate gilt frame; similarly a Victorian print would not suit a thin, pastel-coloured, modern frame. So choose your frame to suit the subject.

Having said all this, when a reasonable degree of practical competence has been achieved, there is no reason why you should not experiment a little and explore the many possibilities that most subjects can offer.

1

Tools and Materials

WORKSHOP LAYOUT

You do not need acres of space in order to start picture framing, but it helps to have a working area that allows you to establish a logical flow from one process to the next. Organize yourself so that you have defined areas for each process, beginning with mitre cutting, then frame jointing, followed by glass cutting, mounting and mount decoration, and finally on to final assembly and finishing of the frame.

However, you do need a reasonably sturdy work surface measuring approximately 4 × 6ft (1.2 × 2m) to which a woodworking vice and a corner clamping vice can be attached. It will also be an advantage if there is additional space that can be used when mitring long lengths of moulding; an open doorway offers this facility.

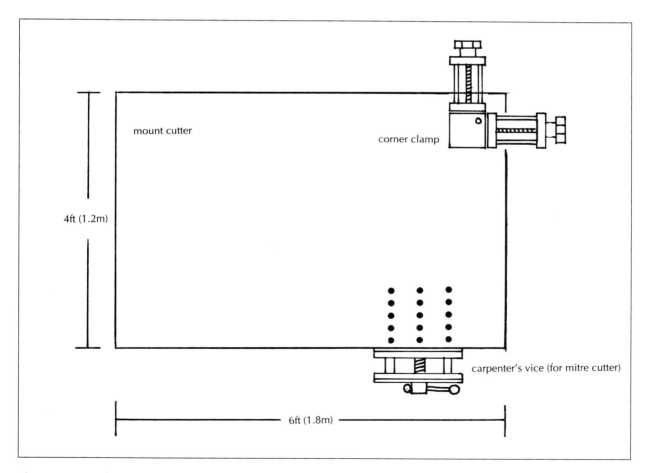

The minimum work surface required.

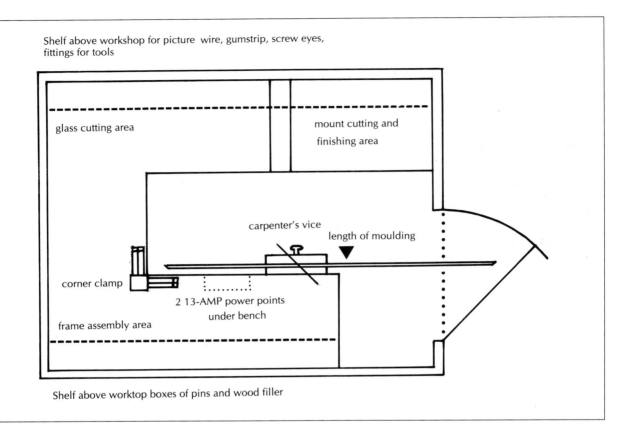

Shelf above workshop for picture wire, gumstrip, screw eyes, fittings for tools

glass cutting area

mount cutting and finishing area

carpenter's vice

length of moulding

corner clamp

2 13-AMP power points under bench

frame assembly area

Shelf above worktop boxes of pins and wood filler

Workshop layout.

Mitring and Assembly Area

The frame mitring and assembly area needs to be well thought out. In particular, the siting of the corner clamping vice is very important. It should be positioned to provide enough room to permit the assembly of frames up to 3 × 4ft (1 × 1.2m). Frames of greater dimensions than these are the exception rather than the rule. Close to the vice should be storage for the following:

● Woodworking adhesive
● Pin hammer
● Punch
● Various-sized pins for securing the joint
● Try square (for checking the accuracy of your cutting and joining)
● A selection of wood fillers to fill over the pin heads

WOOD FILLERS

These come in various forms, mainly creams, wax filler sticks, retouch crayons and joint filler. Retouch creams are soft waxes for touching up frame damage, and are available in many colours which can be mixed to obtain the correct shade. Apply them with a soft cloth or an artist's spatula, leave to harden and then buff with a soft cloth.

Wax filler sticks are very easy to use – simply shave off a small piece and knead it between your fingers until it is pliable. Then press it into the pin hole, leave for a few minutes and then buff with a cotton cloth.

Retouch crayons are wax pencils which are used in a similar way to wax filler sticks.

Joint filler is used to conceal pins punched below the surface of the moulding and for joint filling. It is available in twenty-four colours ranging from white to black, from silver to the many shades of gold and from light oak to dark mahogany. It is applied by the methods described previously.

The corner clamping vice held in a carpenter's vice as an alternative to permanent fixing to the work surface.

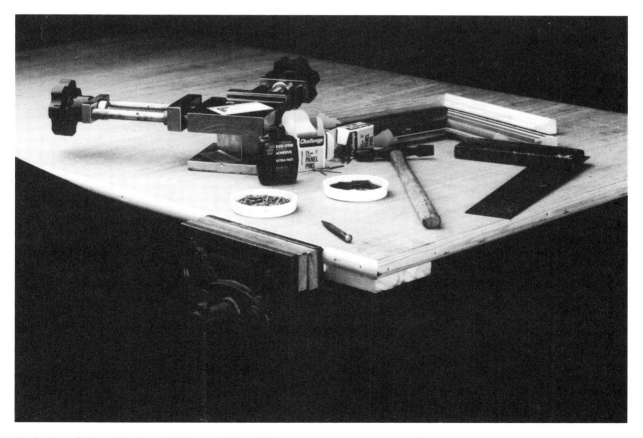

A selection of pins and tools needed to assemble moulding.

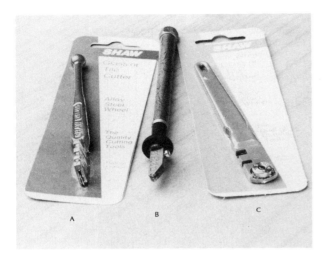

Types of glass cutter: (a) single wheel; (b) oil reservoir; (c) multiwheel.

A self-healing cutting mat with grey board as an alternative.

Glass-Cutting Area

The glass-cutting area needs to be covered with a soft yet firm material; if you can find an offcut of reasonable size of kitchen floor covering such as Flotec or similar, this is ideal. Alternatively, your local glass merchant will be able to supply you with the product they use, although this can be quite expensive. It is vital to vacuum this area regularly to get rid of the slivers of glass which are inevitably a result of the glass-cutting process; these will not only find their way unerringly into your fingers, the larger pieces will scratch the surface of the glass and ruin it.

It is also a good idea to have a small jar with a piece of felt or similar material placed in the bottom and impregnated with light oil to stand your glass cutter in; this will extend the life of the cutting wheels and ensure a clean cut.

You will find the oil reservoir type of cutter is excellent and lasts infinitely longer; I had one in daily use for four years and only had to replace the cutting head when a student tried to re-score a cut after the piece of glass he was trying to cut refused to snap.

Mount-Cutting Area

A self-healing cutting mat is the ideal surface on which to carry out the mount-cutting operation. Failing this, a sheet of 2.5mm framer's grey board will do the job, although it will need replacing frequently to ensure clean edges on your mounts.

Finishing Area

The finishing area should also have a soft surface, as some of the gold finishes in particular are quite delicate and easily damaged. A batten 2 × 1in (50 × 25mm) and 2ft (0.6m) in length should be placed to serve as a stop to rest the frame against when fixing the backing board: this should be firmly fixed, and covered to protect the moulding.

--- TIP ---

A shelf to store the various pins, tapes, screw eyes and picture wire or cord will prove very useful.

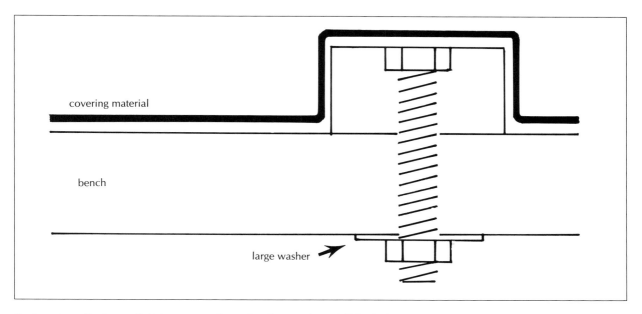

Section view of batten on finishing-area worktop, showing countersunk fixing bolt.

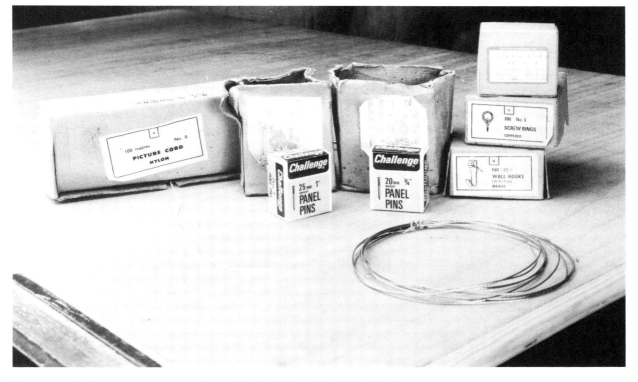

Pins, picture hooks, screw-eyes, picture wire and cord, which need to be kept handy.

POWER SUPPLY

The power supply for your electric drill should be positioned so that it can reach the frame assembly and the frame finishing areas easily, without having to be unplugged.

Lighting

In general, lighting is provided by overhead fluorescent fittings; daylight or colour-matching tubes are best, as they give accurate colours. These can be supplemented with an adjustable desk lamp for close work.

Heating

Heating is a very important consideration. An even temperature is always to be preferred, provided by a reasonably dry source such as electricity. The very damp heat given off by portable bottled gas is not suitable at all, the reason being that paper absorbs small quantities of moisture, as do tapestry and embroideries;

when these are placed behind glass the absorbed moisture can then encourage mould growth and the results will obviously be disastrous, particularly if the artwork is valuable.

TIP

If your framing workshop is an outside studio and too costly to heat for a winter evening's frame making, it is a good idea to make just the frames, and cut the glass there, and to carry out the mounting and finishing in the warmth of the kitchen or other dust-free environment.

ESSENTIAL EQUIPMENT

Before we begin frame making it is essential to have the necessary tools to hand; there is nothing worse than starting work only to find that some vital piece of equipment is missing. I expect you will have most of the following in your toolbox already:

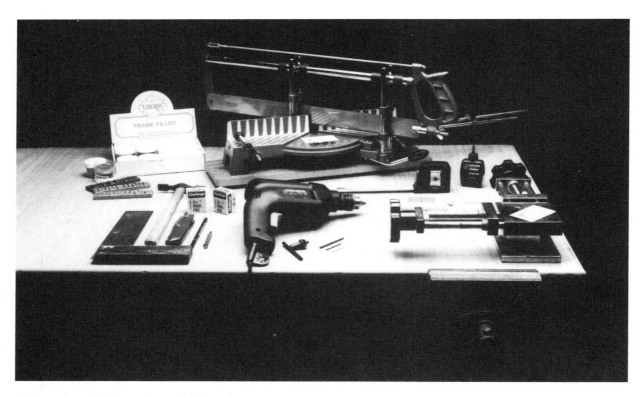

All the tools needed for cutting and jointing a frame.

- 6ft (2m) extending rule
- 2B pencil
- Fine-toothed tenon saw and mitre block, *or* A combined saw and mitre block
- Carpenter's bench vice
- Sharp knife
- Woodworking adhesive
- Corner clamping vice
- Electric drill with a variable speed trigger
- 1mm twist drill
- 3½oz (100g) pin hammer
- Pin punch
- Carpenter's or engineer's try square
- Pins of various lengths
- Set of frame clamps
- Wood fillers of different colours

Using the Mitre Saw

Do practise using the mitre saw, always cutting from the inner edge (shorter) to the back edge (longer) of the moulding. Try cutting short lengths of 2 or 3in (50 or 76mm), then place them in the corner clamping vice and check the fit until you are proficient at cutting the angles and obtaining a tight-fitting joint. Don't forget to inspect the back edge of your moulding which should also be a tight fit.

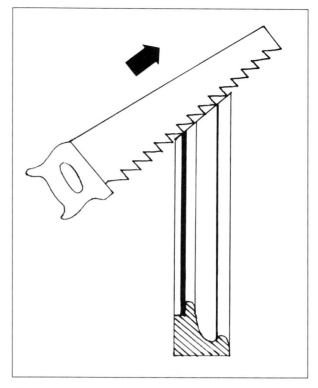

Direction of cut.

An example of a good tight joint.

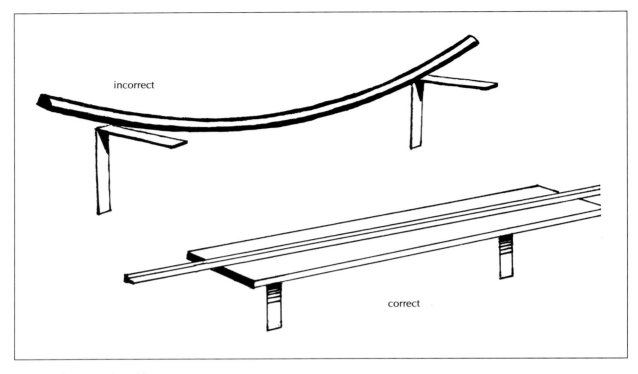

Horizontal storage of moulding.

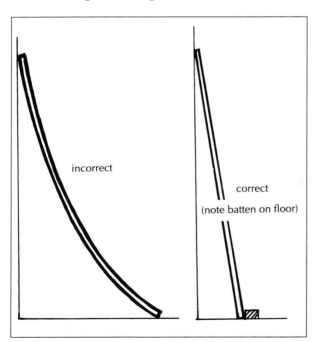

Vertical storage of moulding.

SUMMARY

You now have all the information to set up the frame-making section of your workshop. Laid out carefully and logically in this way, you will be much better able to produce frames quickly and efficiently; this in itself will give beginners in particular the confidence to tackle work of greater complexity.

2

Making a Frame

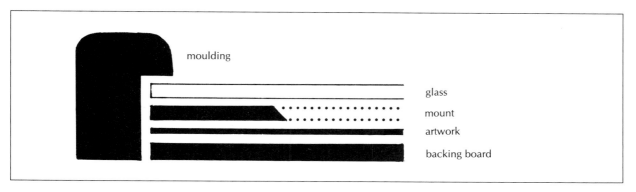

Section through the components of a frame.

moulding

glass

mount

artwork

backing board

Moulding sample held against a picture for appraisal.

CUTTING MITRES

As we have said, it is essential to practise cutting mitres before attempting to make a frame. A very useful exercise is to visit your local frame shop; browse through their stock and select six mouldings in order to purchase offcuts of approximately 2ft (0.6m) in length. Cut these into two 9in (230mm) pieces, mitre them at each end and then join them, making corners; these can be placed against a picture for appraisal. As you buy more lengths of moulding this operation can be repeated and each sample given a reference number, marked on the reverse.

Choose the mouldings carefully, selecting a range to cover the different types you will need to carry out most framing jobs. For example you should have a small gold for watercolours, a small pine cushion for embroideries, a Hogarth for antiquarian prints and maps, and a moulding with a deep rebate which will be ideal for tapestries or stretched oils. Also pick a 1¼in (32mm) wide moulding and one 2in (50mm) wide to suit prints. These can be supplemented at a later date with small dark wood mouldings for photographs. Most manufacturers produce mouldings of a particular profile in several colour variations; this is a great help as you can usually find one colour from the range which will suit a particular picture. Have a 1in (25mm) gold available to frame oils and also mirrors which can be cut to size by your glass supplier.

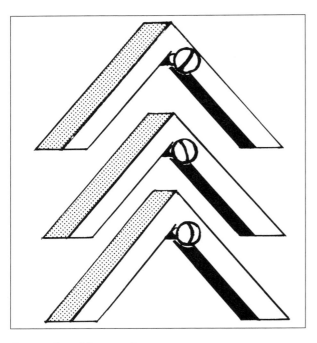

Storage of moulding samples.

Combined saw and mitre block.

Left-Hand Mitres

Now to the task of mitring a piece of moulding: I always use a combined saw and mitre block as they are far more rigid and the work can be held more tightly, giving a more accurate cut and therefore a more tightly fitting joint.

Step 1 Place the mitre block into the carpenter's bench vice and tighten until you can make a firm cut without the block wobbling.

Step 2 With the blade locked up and in the 90° cut position, place your piece of moulding with the back edge against the upright stop.

Saw and mitre held in the carpenter's vice.

Close-up of the mitre block showing the blade locked up.

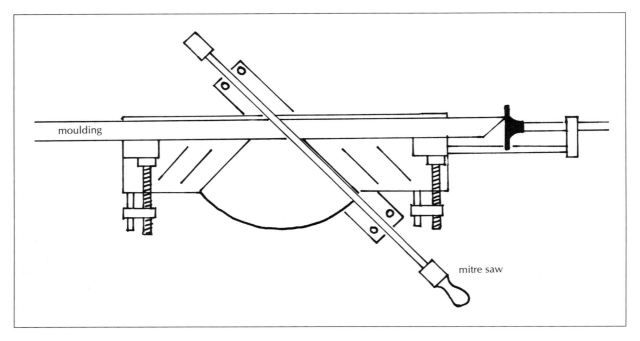

Plan view of moulding in mitre cutter.

Cutting a right-hand mitre.

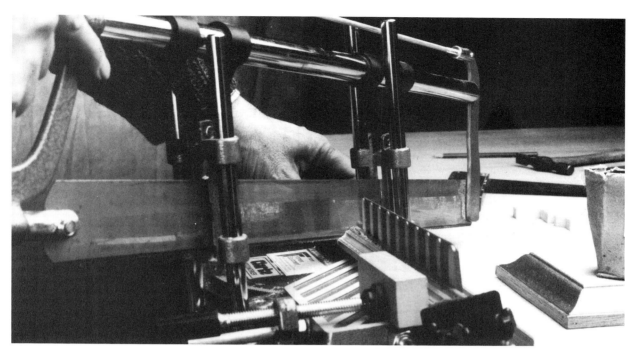

Cutting a left-hand mitre.

Step 3   With the inner or sight edge facing you, slide it to the right until it is just past the blade, then tighten the clamp so the moulding is held firmly; you will probably need a spacing piece to prevent the moulding twisting.
Step 4   Reset the blade to cut a 45° angle from the left-hand side; release the blade locks, and gently lower it to come into contact with the moulding.
Step 5   Make the cut.

Let the weight of the saw apply the downward pressure; *never* force the saw through the moulding as this will result in an inaccurate mitre and will damage the moulding. Try to achieve a smooth forwards and backwards action – this may take slightly longer but will result in a more accurate mitre. Remember that the smoother the mitre, the better your finished joint will be, resulting in less filling and greater satisfaction with the finished frame.

Mitre saw blade set at 90 degrees.

Measuring to the length gauge.

Right-Hand Mitre

To cut the right-hand mitre, release the moulding and reset the blade to the 90° setting. To cut a piece 9in (230mm) long overall, proceed as follows:

Step 1   Measure from the blade to the right-hand stop on the length gauge and lock it firmly; this allows you to cut the next piece to the identical length without re-measuring.
Step 2   Re-set the blade to the right, then release the blade locking clamps and carefully cut the mitre.

Repeat these steps to make two identical lengths ready to join and make your first sample corner.

TIPS

The process of mitring may sound complicated and off-putting but when you actually come to carry out this operation everything will fall into place and you will find it quite straightforward. Always double check your measurements before cutting and always use a sharp saw to be certain of the best possible cut – you will find great difficulty in making a tight-fitting joint if you use a blunt saw. A well cut joint should not need any filler (other than to cover the pin heads).

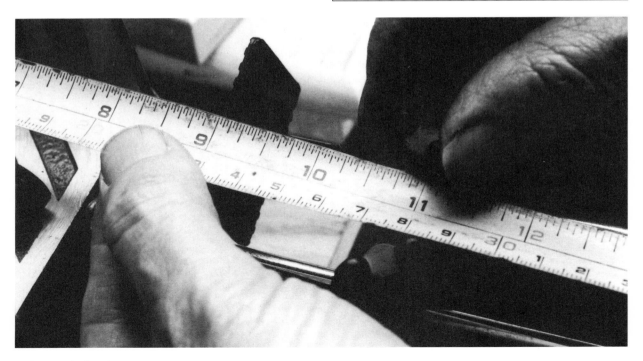

Tightening the length gauge.

Checking two pieces for identical length.

Cleaning Up

Before we progress and make the joint we must be certain that the cut edges are clean, and that there are no pieces of swarf which can settle into the joint and prevent a good fit. To remove these, rub the mitred end on the reverse side of a piece of hardboard; this is abrasive enough to clean up the mitre without making it too loose a fit. Next cut a small piece from the underside of the rebate, starting at the sight edge and cutting back towards the moulding; this is where the majority of obstructions occur. It also makes a small reservoir to collect any excess adhesive squeezed from the joint when clamped.

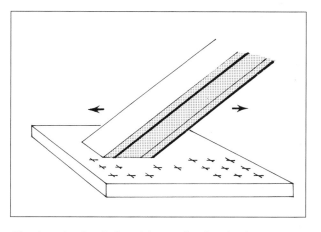

Cleaning mitred end of moulding on dimple side of hardboard.

ADHESIVES

I find that PVA woodworking adhesive is ideal. Do not use adhesives which come in two parts and need mixing: this sort gives a very strong joint, but they are inclined also to give a thick joint which is not suitable to frame making. Therefore choose any of the ready-to-use proprietary brands and you will make strong joints.

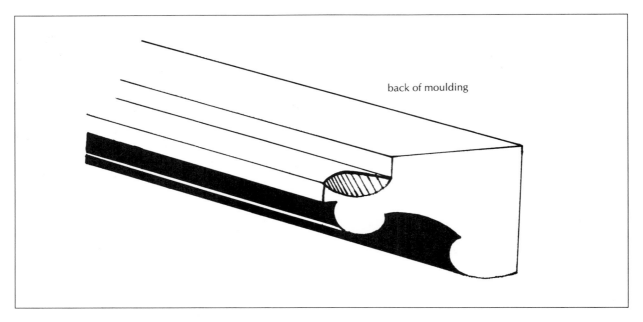

Mitre corner showing cut-out with knife.

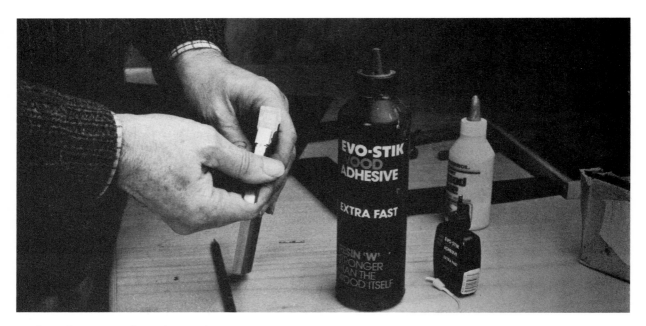

Applying glue to one surface to be joined.

MAKING JOINTS

Before using the corner clamping vice it is advisable to fit card protectors to the clamp faces; this prevents damage to the moulding caused by the hard jaws crushing the timber.

Clamping and Fitting

Step 1   Place one of your mitred pieces in the corner clamp and adjust the pressure until the piece is just held.

Step 2   Place the other piece in the clamp and make the necessary adjustments until the best join is made; with the carpenter's try square, check the accuracy of your work.

Step 3   When you are satisfied, remove one of the pieces and give the mitre face a thin coat of adhesive.

Step 4   Replace in the clamp and retighten, making one final check that the joint is square. Do not forget that the back edge of the joint must also be tight-fitting from top to bottom.

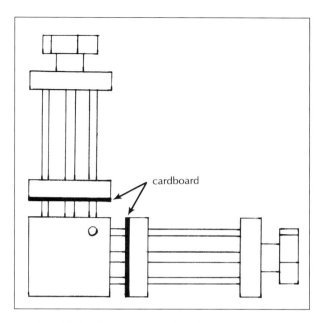

Cardboard facing for corner clamping vice.

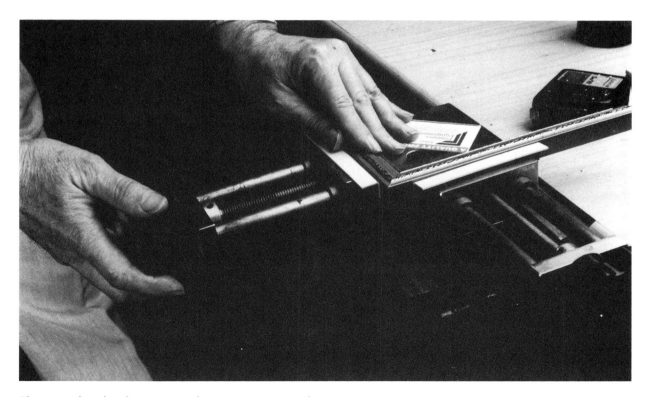

Placement of two lengths in a corner clamping vice. (Note card protectors.)

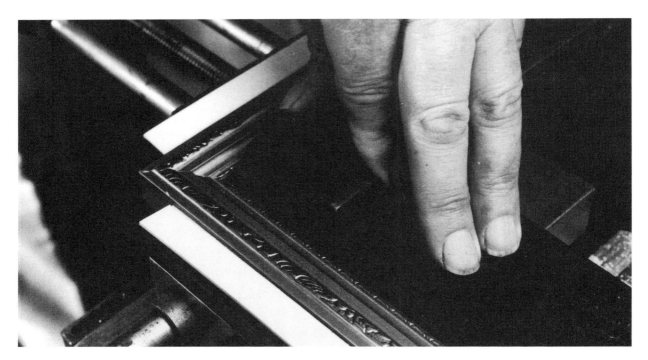

Checking with a try-square the accuracy of the joint after final tightening.

Make sure the back edge is square and tight.

Drilling and Pinning

We are now ready to drill and pin. As a rule-of-thumb guide as to which length pin to use, I find that the pin length and the moulding width should roughly equate, up to a maximum of 2in (50mm). Thus, if you are using a ½in (12mm) moulding, then a ½in (12mm) pin is the correct length to use. Here, I have used 1in (25mm) wide moulding, so will use a 1in (25mm) pin.

Step 1   Drill a 1mm hole approximately ¾in (15mm) deep on either side of the corner, making sure that one is at the front edge and the other at the back edge; this is so the pins will not touch each other inside. Small mouldings up to 1in (25mm) need one pin each side of the joint; those of medium size, up to 2½in (60mm), need two pins in the top and bottom corners through the vertical into the horizontal, and one pin through the horizontal into the vertical. Mouldings 4in (100mm) wide need four pins in each corner.

Step 2   Drive a pin into each hole, stopping before the pins become flush with the moulding so you do not mark the moulding; drive them in with the pin punch until they are just below the surface.

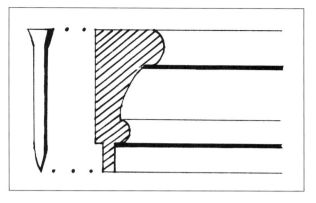

Ensure that the fixing pin is the same depth as the moulding.

You have now completed your first sample corner.

—————————————————— TIP ——————————————————
I cannot stress enough the importance of practising cutting mitres. Following the procedure described, make several sample corners and you will soon become proficient in mitring.

Drilling the hole in preparation for pinning.

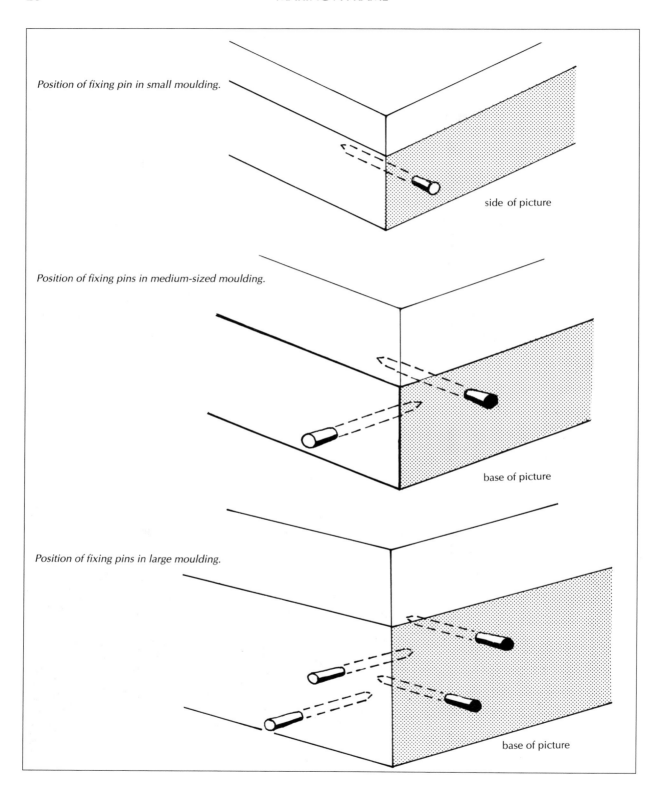

Position of fixing pin in small moulding.

side of picture

Position of fixing pins in medium-sized moulding.

base of picture

Position of fixing pins in large moulding.

base of picture

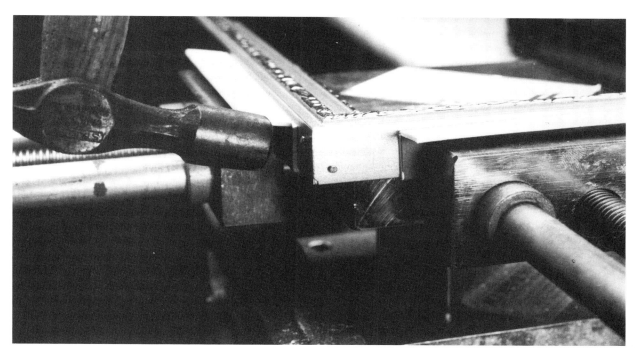

The depth to which pins must be driven in, prior to punching below the surface.

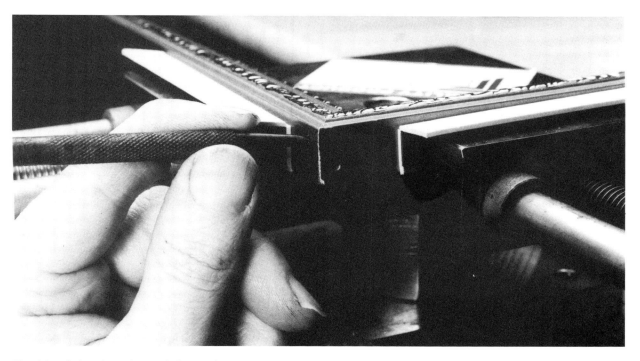

Pins driven below the surface with the punch.

MAKING THE FRAME

We will now make a frame. The moulding I am using here is ¾in (15mm) wide, charcoal coloured, high gloss, and is going to frame an 8 × 10in (205 × 255mm) photograph in a folder. This moulding has been chosen because the photographic folder is charcoal, and the high gloss will form a bright edge which will hold the eye of the person looking at it, and stop it wandering from the subject.

An alternative moulding for framing photographs is a ½in (12mm) walnut or other dark wood with a gold sight line to hold the eye. It is always worth experimenting because half the fun of framing is unexpectedly finding a combination of picture and moulding that blend together perfectly.

Checking the suitability of a moulding and a picture.

Calculating Size

Measuring the folder tells us that we need the frame 10 × 12in (255 × 305mm), so we must make a simple calculation to determine the length of moulding needed. I use the following formula:

length × 2
plus breadth × 2
plus 8 times the moulding width

so using this we have:

12in (300mm) × 2 = 24in (600mm)
plus 10in (250mm) × 2 = 20in (500mm)
plus ¾in (15mm) × 8 = 6in (150mm)
giving 24 + 20 + 6in (600 + 500 + 150mm)
= 50in (1,250mm)

This leaves no room for error, so 60in (1,520mm) would be the amount to buy; also you may find suppliers reluctant to sell a 50in (1,250mm) piece – in fact they might not wish to supply even a 60in (1,520mm) piece and insist you buy a full length, these varying from 6ft (1.8m) to 10ft (3m). Offcuts can be stored for future use.

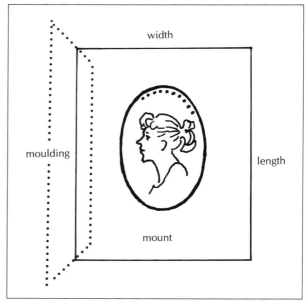

Calculating the amount of moulding needed.

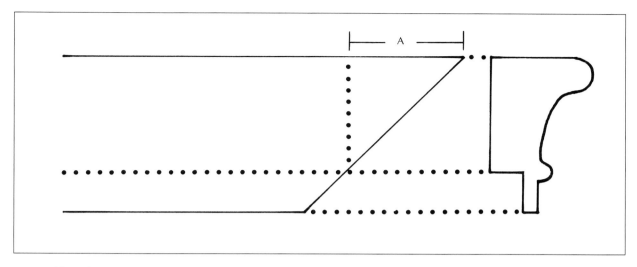

Cut moulding, showing extra length (A), to be allowed for at corners.

Cutting the Mitres

Using the method described earlier, cut the first mitre: the measurement we now need is 12in (300mm) and refers to the inner dimension. To calculate the extra amount needed, measure from the back edge of the moulding to the rebate, in this case ½in (12mm); multiply by 2, as there are two ends, giving 1in (25mm), and add this to the length of your piece to be framed: thus to 12in (300mm), this gives an overall length of 13in (325mm). Set the length gauge to the required measurement and cut two pieces; then re-adjust the gauge and cut the two short sides. After cleaning any swarf from the cut ends, place the four pieces by the corner clamp arranged alternately long and short: this helps to avoid any mix-ups resulting in two long or two short lengths being joined inadvertently.

Should a mix-up occur, do not despair because the joint can be gently prised apart before the glue has set. Take care not to damage the joint face. Then remove the pins. The glue will have to be cleaned off with a damp cloth. Then proceed as above: re-glue and make the joint with the pieces in the correct order. You may need to re-drill the pin holes in a different position or alternatively use slightly longer and thicker pins.

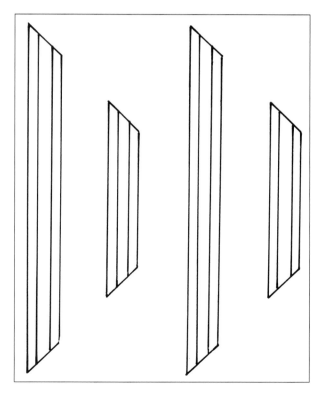

Arrangement of moulding pieces on worktop before assembly.

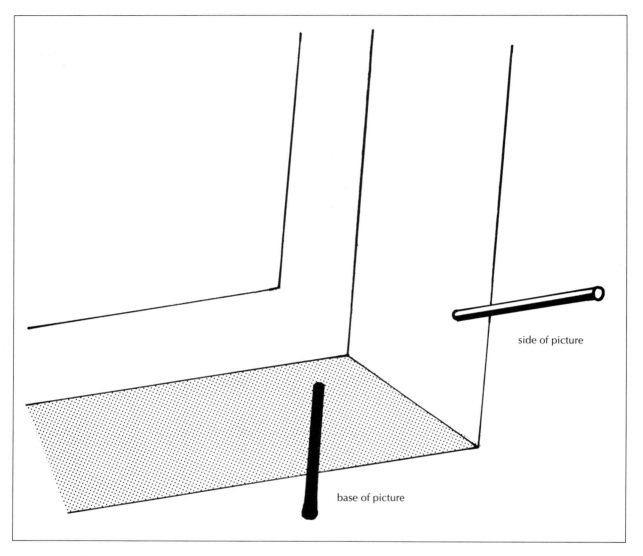

side of picture

base of picture

Arrangement of pins.

Gluing, Drilling and Pinning

Follow the gluing, drilling and pinning procedure, checking for true 90° corners as you progress. A good way of making the pins less noticeable is to place them to the front edge on the top and bottom edges, and the back edge on the sides: positioned like this they will be less visible. It is advisable to place the frame in a set of frame clamps until the joints have set; a few hours should be sufficient, but overnight is better.

Completed frame held firm in the frame clamps until the joints have set.

Putting filler in the pin holes.

Finishing Off

All that remains now is to fill over the pins with filler. You will need several shades: these can be mixed to obtain a good match, then pressed in with an artist's spatula and gently rubbed down with extra fine sandpaper when dry. You now have a frame ready for glazing.

3

Glass and Glass Cutting

TOOLS AND MATERIALS

The glass-cutting operation seems to cause more anxiety than any other, and yet to my mind it is one of the easiest. The secret is confidence: glass when handled correctly and carefully is quite safe. However, there are obvious pitfalls to avoid and I shall comment on these as we come across them, rather than list them here.

The ideal working surface for glass cutting has already been described in an earlier chapter, so I am assuming you have prepared a clear, flat area and have covered it appropriately.

TOOLS AND EQUIPMENT

The items needed for glass cutting are as follows:

- Rule
- Fine-point, water-soluble pen
- T-square approximately 3ft (1m) long
- Glass cutter
- Pliers
- Glass cleaner and cloths
- Safety glasses
- First-aid kit

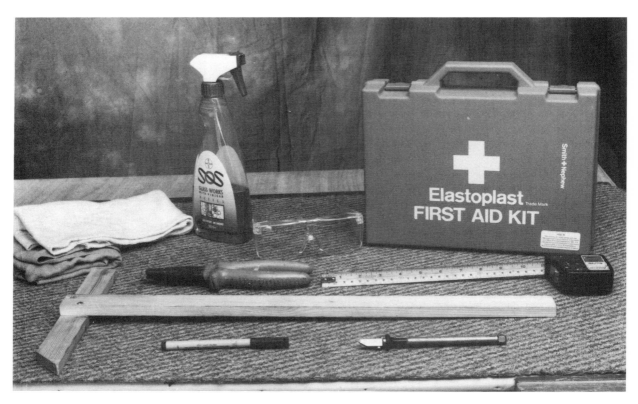

All the items needed for glass cutting.

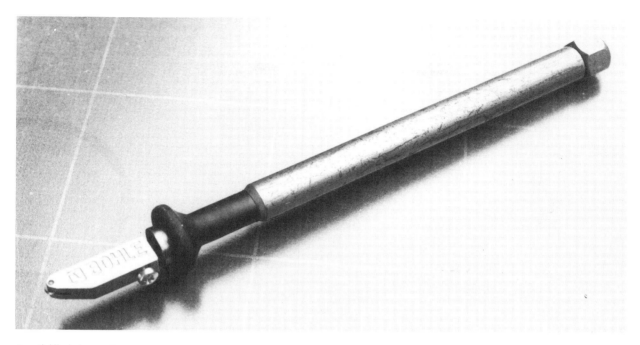

An oil-filled glass cutter.

Glass Quality

I use 2mm float glass made by Pilkington; I find this very reliable, by which I mean that it cuts true and has no waves or seeds. In the past I have been supplied with imported 'float' glass, and found that it had seeds in, and that it broke anywhere except where it had been scored, a problem I have never encountered since changing to the British product.

Glass Cutters

The sort of cutter I prefer to use has an oil reservoir that keeps the cutting wheel lightly lubricated; this ensures a long wheel life and accurate cutting. The multi-wheel types work just as well provided they are properly cared for: it is best to store them in a small jar with an oil-impregnated pad placed in the bottom, as this ensures that the cutting wheel is always lubricated. Too much oil on the pad will not do any harm, but it will leave a residue along the cut edge which must be removed immediately so it doesn't transfer to the work being framed, causing damage.

Glass cutter in a jar with oil impregnated material to keep the cutting wheel lubricated.

The T-Square

I made my own T-square from 2 × 1in (50 × 25mm) planed timber, the short side 12in (300mm), and 3ft (1m) in length. Obviously the chosen timber was straight and true, and the advantage with my square lies in its thickness: the cutter has to be as upright as possible to make a clean cut, and I found drawing-board squares too thin; my cutter wavered too much for my comfort, and the extra thickness of 2 × 1in (50 × 25mm) timber gave me better vertical support.

HOW TO MAKE YOUR OWN T-SQUARE

From a 4ft (1.2m) length of 2 × 1in (50 × 25mm) straight timber cut a piece 12in (300mm) long. Half-way along this piece position the remaining 3ft (1m) length. Check with your try square that it forms a 90° angle, and then mark each side with a pencil. The next step is to drill two ³⁄₁₆ (4mm) holes at the end of the 3ft (1m) piece for the fixing screws. After cleaning away any swarf and countersinking these holes, apply a coat of adhesive between the pencil lines marked on the shorter piece, and fix the two pieces with one screw, checking that it is square before tightening fully. Once you are entirely satisfied with the accuracy, insert the second screw and tighten fully.

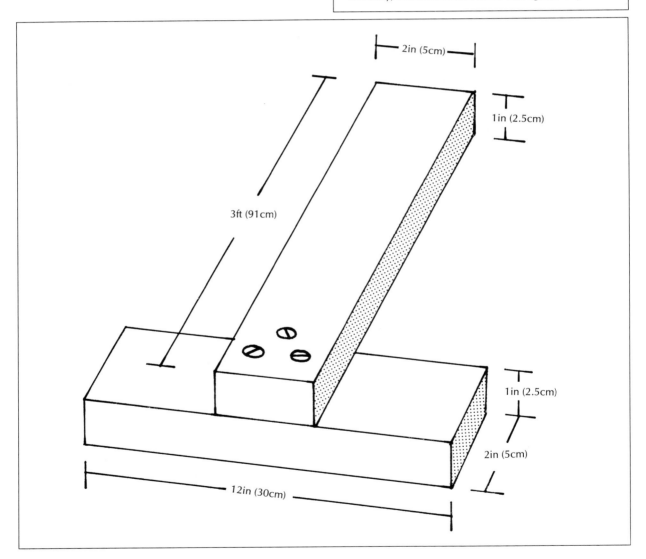

A glass-cutting T-square (not to scale).

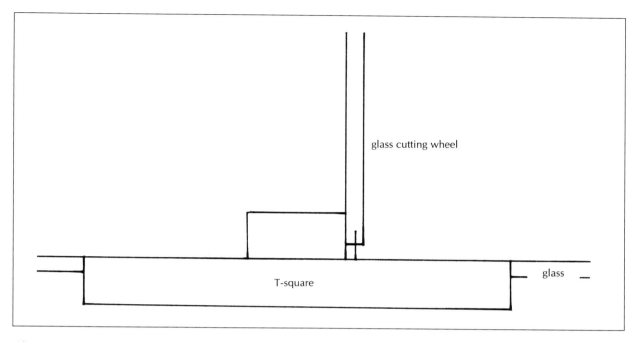

Glass cutting using correct 2 × 1in (5 × 2.5cm) T-square.

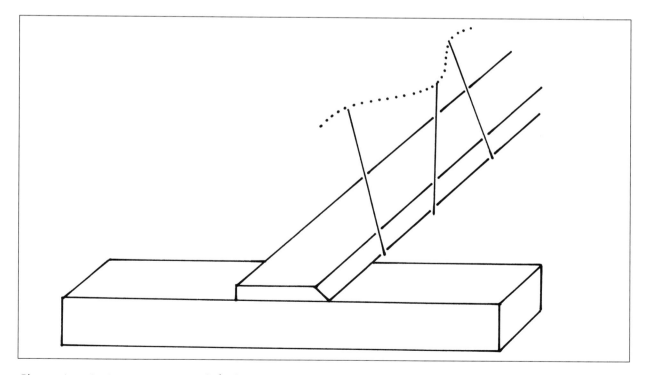

Glass cutting using incorrect T-square, which allows cutting wheel to waver.

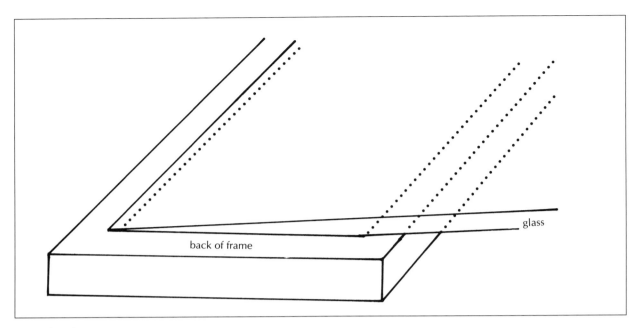

Measuring glass.

CALCULATING THE SIZE OF GLASS REQUIRED

There are two ways of assessing the size of glass needed:

Step 1 Measure the aperture in the frame, then mark the sheet of glass with a water soluble pen; remember to reduce the dimensions by about ⅛in (3mm), which will give a comfortable fit without being sloppy. This is the method I use when cutting a small piece from a full sheet.
Step 2 The second method is to place the frame under the glass with one corner fitted into the moulding, then mark the cutting line directly without measuring.

SAFETY

Always keep a first aid kit handy; these can be bought from your local chemist, or you can assemble a selection of waterproof plasters, antiseptic cream, tweezers and cotton wool ready for any emergency. If an accident occurs and blood from a cut gets on a print or water-colour place the stained article in a tray of distilled water immediately and leave to soak for at least twenty-four hours; do *not* agitate the water or use a brush to remove the stain. After twenty-four hours gently remove the picture from the bath, lifting it by the corners of the longest side; allow the excess water to drain off and place it face up on a clean piece of white blotting paper to dry. This should remove the stain – if it does not the picture will need the attention of a skilled restorer.

This is a useful technique when for example the piece of glass needs a small amount removing to fit.

GLASS-CUTTING PROCEDURE

Having established the size of glass required and marked where the cuts are to be made, the first thing to do is to put on your safety glasses. Then proceed as follows:

Step 1 Slide the glass to the edge of the work surface and place the cutting wheel on the first mark; then slide the T-square up to the cutter. I find that downward pressure on the T-square placed roughly centrally on the glass is sufficient to prevent lateral movement.
Step 2 Holding the glass cutter as you would a pen, move it to the edge furthest from you, and with firm downward pressure draw it smoothly towards you, making sure the cut is from edge to edge. If the cut is not continuous do not try to re-cut over again, as this will ruin the cutter wheel; it is better to re-score slightly inside your first attempt.
Step 3 Place a thin object, such as a ruler, under the cut and press down firmly on each side; the glass should snap cleanly.

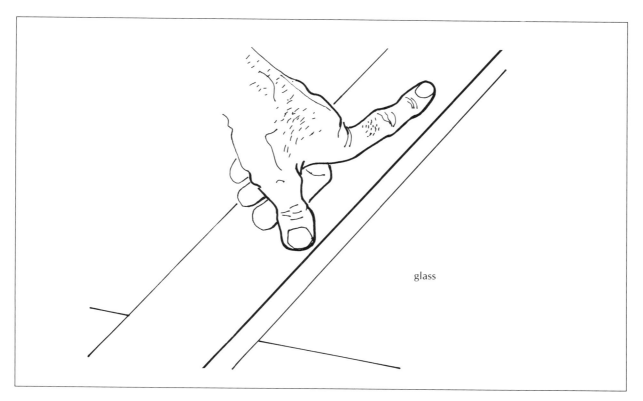

glass

How to hold the T-square steady.

Ruler placed under the glass prior to snapping the glass along the score line.

Cutting Oval and Circular Shapes

The task of cutting oval and circular pieces is only marginally more difficult:

Step 1   Cut a piece of glass approximately 2in (50mm) bigger than the oval or circular frame.

Step 2   Turn the frame face down and place the glass on it; now make a freehand cut away from you. It is easier to judge the position of the cutter this way. Using the rebate as a guide, you will have to keep breaking off the cut and restarting, carefully picking up the point at which you stopped until a complete circuit is made.

Step 3   Place the cutting wheel in contact with the circular cut, and score to the edge of the glass.

Step 4   Firmly tap the underside of the glass immediately beneath the cut with the cutter until the cut reaches the oval.

Step 5   Continue tapping until you are left with the completed piece of glass, ready to drop in the frame.

There is a definite knack to glass cutting which will come with practice!

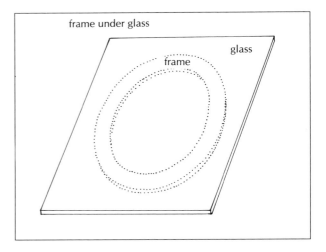

Cutting glass for an oval frame.

——————————————— TIP ———————————————
Once again, practice is the key: obtain some scrap offcuts from your supplier, and practise with small shapes until you achieve satisfactory results.

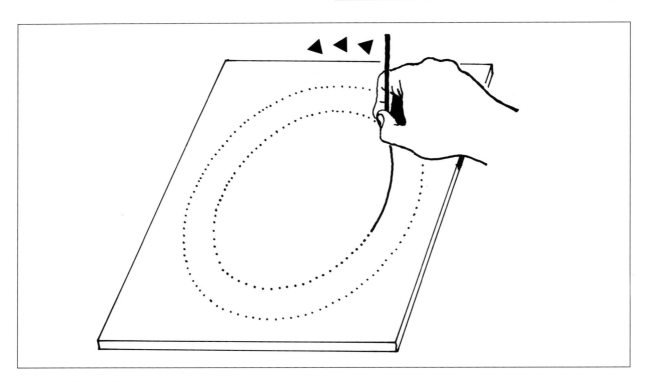

Direction of freehand cut.

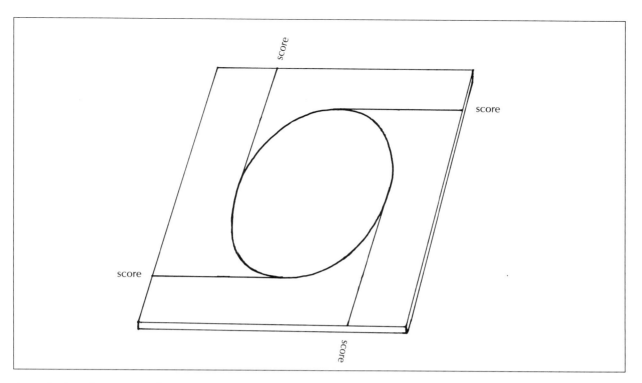

Scores in glass after cutting oval.

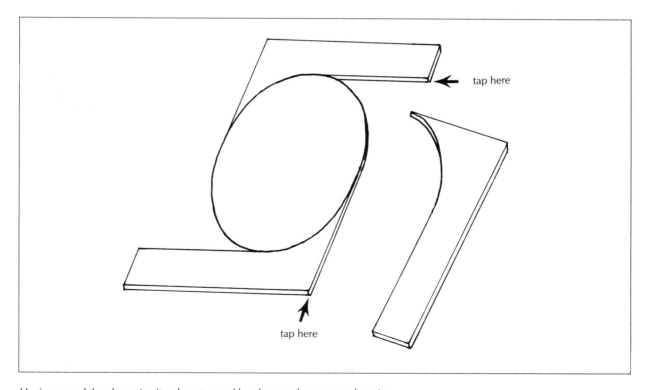

Having scored the glass, give it a sharp tap and break away the unwanted sections.

PLASTIC GLASS

An alternative to glass is plastic glass. I use it for glazing pictures to be hung in a child's room, as it is virtually unbreakable. It cuts very easily, however: just score it with a lino-cutting blade fitted in your Stanley knife, and snap it over the edge of your bench. The safety aspect is our main concern here: if the frame is knocked to the floor the joints may part, but you can be sure that no slivers of glass will be scattered on the carpet. This product needs to be kept free of dust by flicking gently; polishing will scratch the surface.

Plastic glass is made from clear shatter-resistant styrene and is protected on both sides by a polythene film which you peel off after cutting to size. Its ultra-violet stabilizer absorbs many of the wavelengths which cause discolouration of the piece.

Plastic glass comes in two surface finishes, clear and non-glare, and there are special cleaners available which do not damage its soft surface. These are applied with a very soft lint-free cloth.

Scoring plastic glass: three or four passes are sufficient.

Snapping the glass on the edge of the bench.

Removing the protective film from the plastic glass before fitting into the frame.

Dusting the plastic glass with a large soft brush to avoid scratching.

Cleaning glass.

CLEANING GLASS

A few thoughts on glass cleaning before we end this section. Normally I use one of the domestic glass cleaners readily available. However, if the glass is old and heavily stained, I use a solution of 5 parts household ammonia to 100 parts water; I wipe it on and leave it for about two minutes, then polish with a soft cloth. I only use this in extreme cases.

A WORD OF CAUTION

When polishing glass I like to form a pad with my cloth, but it is important to exercise great care when cleaning near the corners: it is very easy to catch the cloth and leave it behind, so your fingers then run unprotected down the edge of the glass, resulting in a nasty cut.

Obviously glass cleaning takes place at the final assembly stage.

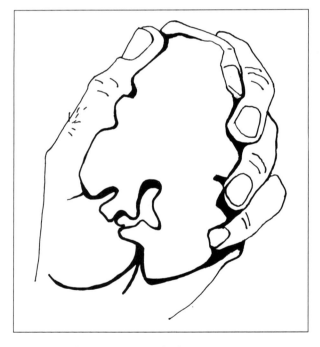

Holding the duster – correct method.

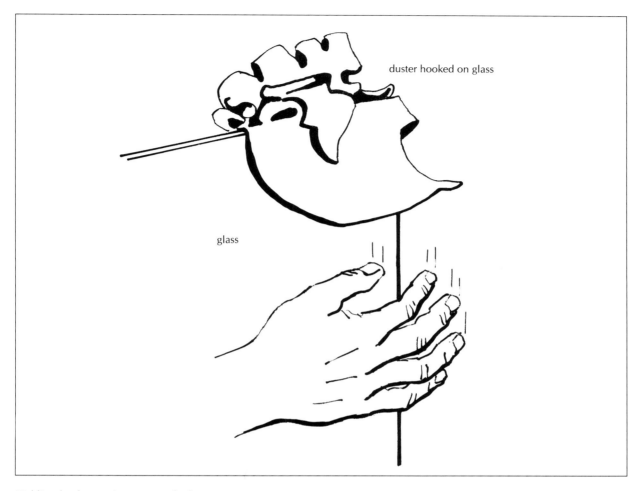

Holding the duster – incorrect method.

DIFFUSED REFLECTION GLASS

As the name implies, this product (often referred to as non-reflective glass) will drastically reduce those annoying reflections created on the glass which prevent a clear view of the picture. The glass has a slightly dimpled surface that breaks up the reflections, but it does not eliminate them totally. It will also mute colours and if the artwork is behind a mount and not in contact with the glass, then the clarity of the picture is reduced.

Sometimes this is not so important, for example, in a soft landscape picture or perhaps a portrait photograph where all the sitter's facial blemishes are visible, where the use of this type of glass is very useful as the effect produced can be very flattering.

A word of warning: do not use diffused glass on any old or valuable artwork, because the dimples can store minute quantities of moisture which can encourage mould growth and damage the artwork.

4

Mounts and Mount Cutting

First I will introduce you to the various types of mount board available, then we will discuss the aesthetics and finally the mechanics of mount cutting.

TOOLS

- An 18in (500mm) rule
- 2B and 4H pencils
- 3ft (1m) length of ¼in (6mm) plate glass 4in (100mm) wide
- Scalpel, replaceable blade type
- Hand-held 45° mount cutter
- Soft cutting surface

These can be supplemented with:
- A Logan compact mat cutter
- A Logan oval and circle cutter

IDENTIFYING MOUNT BOARD

A mount, or a mat, is the name used to describe the material that surrounds, or borders, a picture. They are cut from sheets of special card that is easy to cut, and has a thin coloured paper surface. The range of colours is considerable, the complete spectrum from black to pure white, and there are many surfaces to choose from: most are plain, although textured and fabric ones are becoming more readily available, as are stippled finishes and coloured centres. Some manufacturers produce Ingrès surfaces: these use delicate colours and have thin lines running through them, a particularly useful feature when the need to emphasize length or height is important (depending on their direction, of course).

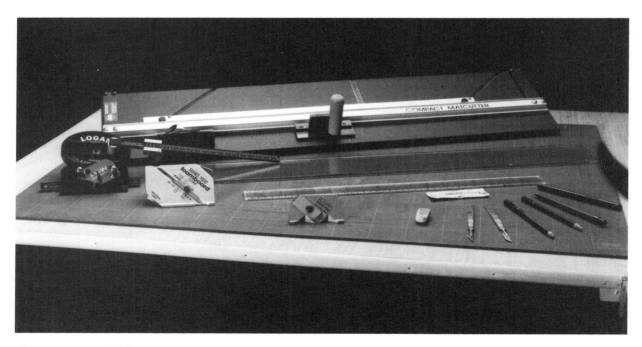

The equipment needed for mount cutting.

A selection of mount board samples.

Samples of Ingres board. (Note the texture lines of the surface paper.)

Sizes and Quality

Mount board comes in the following sizes:

imperial, 32 × 21in (813 × 533mm);
double imperial, 42 × 32in (1,120 × 813mm);
A1, 33 × 23in (841 × 594mm);
A0 46 × 33in (1,188 × 841mm).

There are three thicknesses, 4, 6 and 8 sheet, and these translate into 975, 1,275 and 1,750 microns ± 10 per cent, the most used thickness being 6 sheet. The three main qualities are neutral pH, conservation quality (acid free) and museum quality (acid free). (One micron is one millionth of a metre, and refers here to board thickness.)

PRODUCING MOUNT BOARD

Before we continue I should explain how mount board is made. Cellulose fibres are the basis of chemically made boards and papers; cellulose is the building material in all plant life, although some species of plant produce a more pure form than others. A tree which grows to seventy feet (20m) or more requires many resinous compounds to enable it to continue growing without bending under its own weight or breaking; a low-growing plant on the other hand does not need the same gums and resins. The tree is therefore the most common source of cellulose used for board and paper making, and can be processed in many ways to produce the individual fibres required.

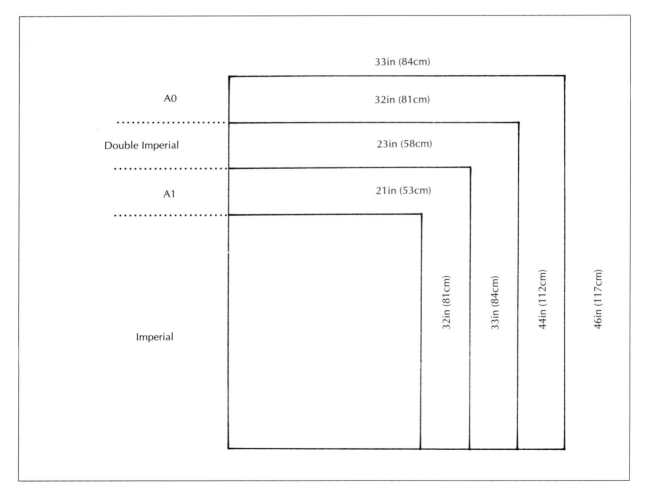

Mount board sizes. (Not to scale.)

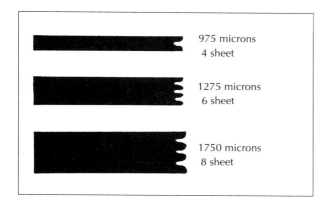

975 microns
4 sheet

1275 microns
6 sheet

1750 microns
8 sheet

Thicknesses of mount board. (Not to scale.)

Types of Woodpulp

The production of **mechanical woodpulp** starts by debarking the tree and grinding the pulp into small pieces. This pulp is full of the resins and other chemicals produced by the growing tree; these resins are known as lignins and are highly acidic. Material produced from this pulp is light-sensitive and will fade and discolour with time; also, being highly acidic, it will become brittle. This effect can be delayed by a process called buffering, which involves adding calcium carbonate (chalk) which ensures any acidic pollution is neutralized when absorbed by the paper. By doing this the degradation can be delayed for months or even years depending on the amount of acidity, the buffer used and the storage conditions.

Another form of pulp is **chemical woodpulp**: this is produced by chipping the whole tree into small pieces approximately 2cm square; these are then treated with chemicals to remove the lignins. This pulp is thus rendered free of acid, it is pure and very white, and because there is no acid present it can last for many decades without changing colour. Chemical pulp has longer fibre lengths and so produces stronger sheets of board.

COTTON

Cotton is the most significant source of cellulose used for producing pulps. It does not produce any lignins as a byproduct of its lifestyle so it is inherently acid free, and will therefore not fade, nor will it become brittle with age. Its fibres are of the very best quality.

Adding Acid

Acid can be added to the pulp during the manufacturing process for many reasons. The problem that it is most often employed to solve is this: some dyes will not bond to the paper fibres and would wash out or produce a blotchy sheet, but using an acid mordant will fix the dye to the fibres, thus giving good, even colour. Usually pale colours do not need acid fixing; the darker the colour the more likely the need for a fixative.

Sizing

Papers are traditionally sized with a rozin/alum medium. Sizing is essential to control the absorbency of the paper – if the paper were to be left unsized it would act like blotting paper. In the latter stages of this process the paper stock is buffered; some of the acid will remain in the fibres and will cause discoloration and brittleness over a long time. This process is known as acid sizing. Sometimes the mill will buffer the paper by adding calcium carbonate; this results in what is known as neutral pH paper. A more modern technique is to use a synthetic called Alkyl Kethene Dimer (AKD) which is a non-acidic sizing medium. This type of size can only be used under neutral conditions and the resulting paper is called neutral sized.

TYPES OF MOUNT BOARD

Neutral pH Mount Board

Most neutral pH boards have three basic components: the surface paper, the centre core and the backing paper. The **surface paper** is made from high quality wood cellulose fibres and is lignin free, producing a neutral pH specification. The **centre core** is made from virgin wood pulp; it is neutral sized, and buffered with calcium carbonate (chalk) which maintains an alkaline pH. This centre cuts cleanly and smoothly and gives an excellent bevel.

The **backing paper** is made from strong sulphate, chemically bleached, cellulose fibres, completely free from lignin. It, too, is neutral sized and buffered with calcium carbonate to maintain an alkaline pH for life.

Conservation Quality Board

Conservation board is produced from 100 per cent chemical woodpulp which is sized using AKD; it has no added pigments or dyes and is a true acid-free board. The white centre gives a smooth clean bevel cut, and remains pure white throughout its life. The backing paper differs from neutral pH board in that it is made from strong, chemically bleached glucose fibres which are completely free from groundwood and contain negligible residual chloride and sulphate ions. This is most important because this is the part of the board which comes into contact with the artwork, and as such could damage archival pieces.

Museum Quality Board

Museum board can be defined as solid coloured boards that have been manufactured from 100 per cent rag (cotton) fibres which give an even colour throughout when bevel cut. The 100 per cent cotton furnish gives the following features: 1) exceptional surface strength to withstand repeated handling; 2) very smooth, clean bevel cuts; 3) freedom from any substance which may affect the permanence of the board: it is acid free, and has a pH of 8.0 ± 0.5 achieved by neutral/alkaline sizing which preserves the archival qualities; 4) it is buffered with calcium carbonate to maintain lifelong pH against atmospheric pollution; (5)

it has a smooth Hot-Pressed finish on the surface and readily accepts wash lines; the reverse has a Not finish.

This board should be used when mounting any artwork of great value because it makes an acid-free environment and gives maximum protection against the atmosphere.

SELECTING A MOUNT

Mount Colour

The first consideration when choosing a mount is its colour: this should be coherent with the frame and the picture, so the eye is led into the picture by the mount, rather than attracted to the mount itself – if the colour of a mount is too strong, it will overpower the picture. Thus as a general rule, try to avoid bright colours; rather, choose neutral or muted tones. There are, however, occasions where contrasts can be very effective: try balancing a warm picture with a cool-toned mount, for example; and watercolours are often mounted in pale colours which are then decorated with wash lines which aim to pick out some of the tones in the picture. An Indian ink line drawing will accept a strong mount colour; maroon or dark green can be particularly effective.

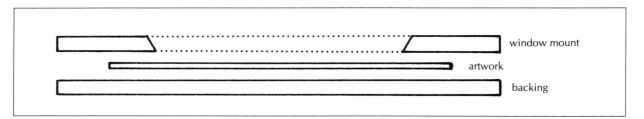

window mount

artwork

backing

Section through artwork and mount.

————————————————— TIPS —————————————————
Artwork on paper should be protected against the environment, but it is equally important that when framed it does not touch the glass, as damp from the glass can transfer impurities to the paper or worse still the image can transfer to the glass. Photographs are particularly prone to sticking to the glass, and the only way to separate the photo from glass is to cut the sticking area carefully with a scalpel. Soaking is quite ineffective; I have had a print in soak for forty-eight hours with no sign of release. A mount therefore plays a vital role as spacer between artwork and glass.

Mount Proportions

The mount proportions are decided next: they need to be wide enough to allow the picture to breathe, but not so wide that the picture looks lost, or so narrow that it looks cramped. It is usual to have the bottom of the mount wider than the top and sides by approximately 20 per cent; this prevents the feeling of the picture falling out of the frame, which would happen if all four sides were of equal width. Various effects can be produced by varying how close the mount is to the picture; thus a ½in (12mm) margin can give a feeling of space and airiness to a landscape, whereas tight mounting can be constrictive.

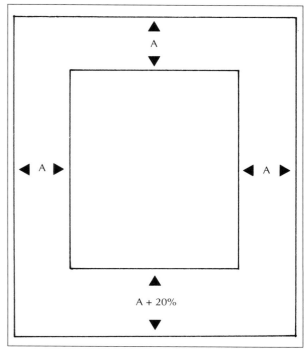

Calculating the width of a mount: the top and both sides should be equal; the bottom should be 20% larger than the other three sides.

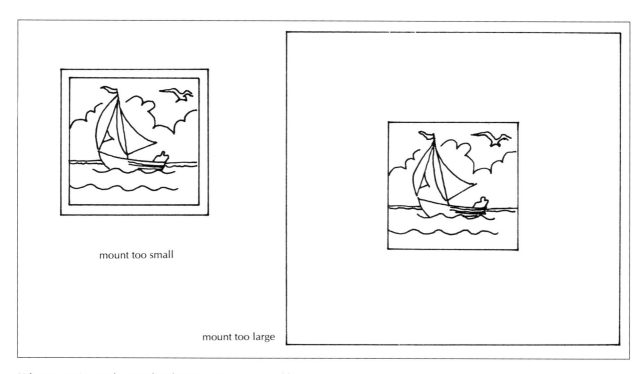

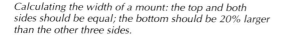

mount too small

mount too large

When mounting, make sure that the proportions are sensible.

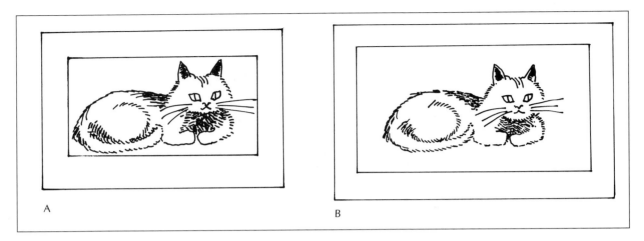

A   B

When calculating the size of the mount, allow background space around the subject. In (a) the mount is too close to the subject, creating a cramped effect. The space around the subject in (b) is much more satisfactory.

Before deciding how much background space to leave around the subject, use L-shaped pieces of cardboard or other firm material to experiment with possible effects.

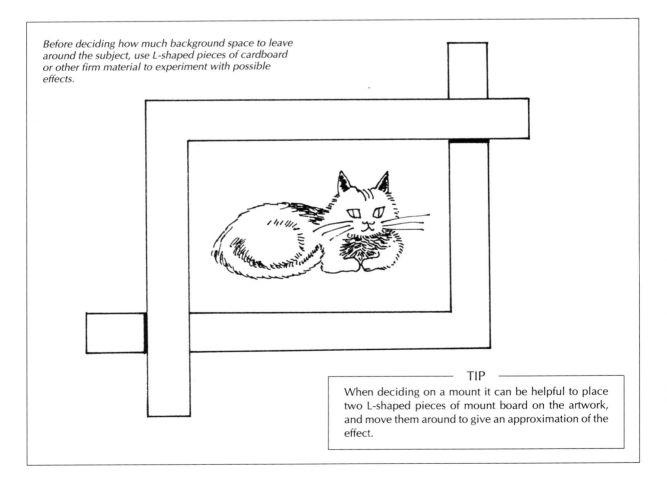

TIP

When deciding on a mount it can be helpful to place two L-shaped pieces of mount board on the artwork, and move them around to give an approximation of the effect.

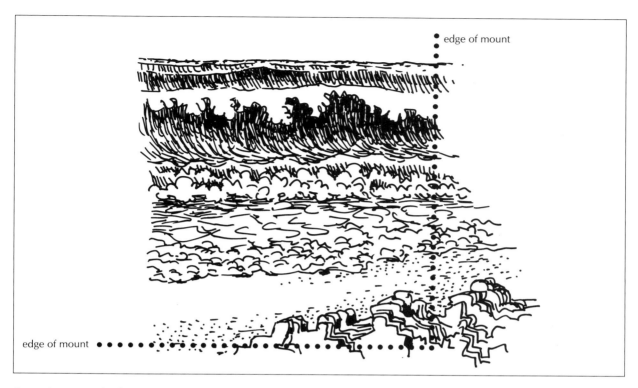

Some pictures need to be cropped because the edges are uneven. In some cases composition can be improved by judicious cropping.

A Double Mount

If the edges of the painting do not lend themselves to display, a feeling of space can be created by the use of a double mount, the inner mount being white or off-white; your chosen mount colour should be cut with a larger aperture to allow ½in (12mm) of white to show.

Using a double mount: the white inner creates a feeling of space.

TIPS

Be creative with your mounts; try double and triple ones. Another technique is to glue together several sheets of board, then bevel cut them to the desired size, thus creating a deep mount. Experiment with colouring the bevel – gilt cream carefully applied with a finger can be most effective (take care not to cut yourself on the bevel). Use colour creatively; avoid obvious combinations occasionally; create interest with pencil and washlines, but be subtle so that your mounts and decorations remain secondary to the picture, enhancing rather than dominating it.

————————————————— EXAMPLE —————————————————

If we were mounting a watercolour of image size 8 × 10in (203 × 254mm) on a piece of watercolour paper 10 × 12in (254 × 304mm), and had decided on top and side widths of 2in (50mm), the bottom would be 2½in (62mm) wide – 2in (50mm) × 20% = 2.4in (62mm). The overall size of board needed is calculated by taking the image length, in this case 10in (254mm), and adding to it the width of the mount, 2in (50mm) each side, making 4in (100 mm), giving a total length of 14in (354mm). Next, take the image height – in this case 8in (203mm) – and add to this the top mount width, 2in (50mm) and the bottom mount width 2½in (62mm): this gives a total measurement of 12½in (316mm). If we were using a double mount we would cut two pieces 14in × 12½in (354 × 316mm): the lower board would have widths of 2in (50mm) for the top and sides, with the base 2½in (62mm); the top board widths of 1½in (38mm) for the top and sides and a base width of 2in (50mm), which will leave a ½in (12mm) strip of the lower board visible; the ½in (12mm) can be variable to suit the picture, and in fact can be made any size you wish. Remember the window size should be smaller than the overall size of the artwork: if it is cut the same size the artwork will fall through; it needs at least an ⅛in (3mm) overlap to be secure.

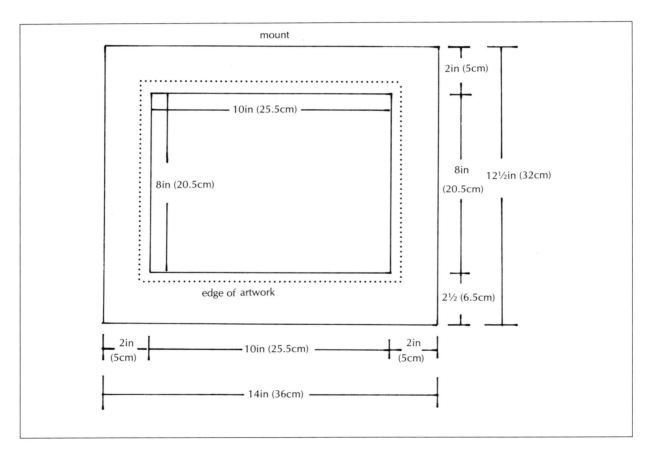

Measuring a mount.

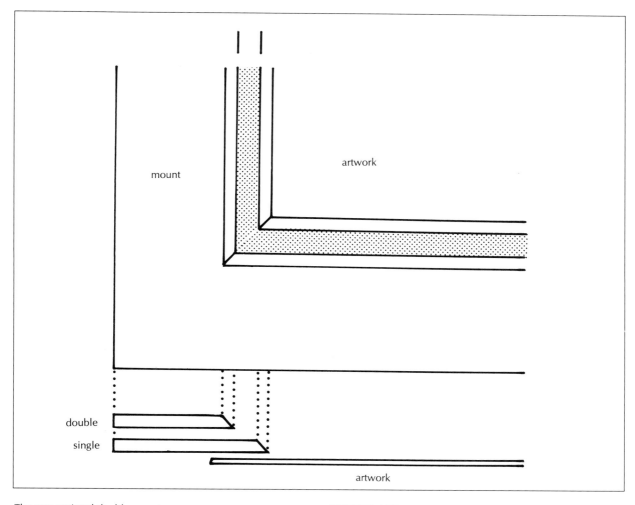

The conventional double mount.

Squaring up the Artwork

The next step is to ensure the artwork is square. Measuring the diagonals will confirm this: if there are discrepancies, then adjustments must be made, particularly if it has been decided to include a white border to give 'breathing space'. This is an instance where the double mount described in the last section can be used; it can be cut to overlap the image sufficiently to give a true area, without encroaching too much and thereby altering the artist's original composition.

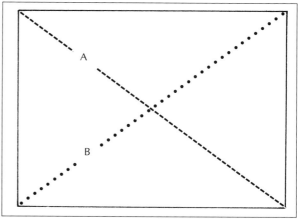

Checking that the picture is square: A should equal B.

Marking the mount aperture on the back of the mount board with a rule and pencil.

Marking Out the Mount

So, we will assume the artwork is perfectly square: taking the watercolour we have used as an example, we know the size of mount board needed is 12½ × 14in (316 × 354mm). Making sure the work surface is clean, place the sheet of mount board face down and consider the most economical way to remove the size of piece required. I always take into account the size of the piece I will be left with; a long, narrow piece of board can be used to cut on, so bear this in mind.

The next step is to mark out the window on the back, using your rule and pencil: keep the borders 2in (50mm) at the top and sides, and 2½in (62mm) at the bottom, again checking everything is square – remember, it is better to measure and check for squareness twice, and to cut once.

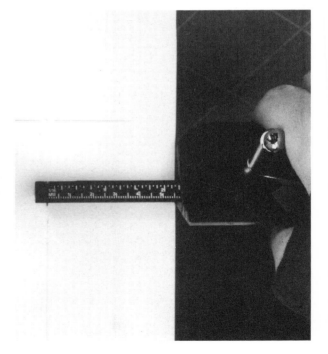

The mount cutter with a built-in marking gauge.

TIP

When marking out, extend the lines at the corners to make the start and finish points of the cut easier to see.

CUTTING OUT THE MOUNT

A Straight-Cut Mount

When you are confident the marking out is correct, place a cutting mat or a piece of scrap card beneath the board to be cut: this will give a cleaner cut, it will protect the work surface and give a longer life to your cutter blade. Using a straight-edge and scalpel, cut along the pencil lines, keeping the scalpel upright; do not try to penetrate the board with a single cut, it is better to make several passes. Take care at the corners not to cut past the mark as it will show on the surface, giving an unprofessional look. When all the sides have been cut and the centre removed, you will have produced a straight-cut mount.

Cutting the mount out of the whole sheet of board.

The finished mount.

A Bevel Mount

I have often read how to cut a bevel mount – a mount where the window is cut at a 45° angle – using a straight-edge and craft knife, but in practice I have never cut a satisfactory bevel by this method. I find it is very difficult to maintain a consistent 45° angle even over a short distance. My answer to this problem is to use one of the hand-held mat cutters; these are quite inexpensive, and once mastered, are reasonably easy to use. I have a 36in (1m) length of ¼in (6mm) plate glass with polished edges, obtained from a local glazier, which allows me to see the pencil marks at the corners so preventing too long a cut. Proceed as follows:

Step 1 Place the straight-edge between the pencil line and the board edge, and make adjustments to bring it against the line.

Step 2 Holding it firmly with your left hand, bring the cutter to the corner nearest to you and press it into the board approximately ⅛in (3mm) before the corner.

Step 3 Then push it smoothly away from you, finishing the cut approximately ⅛in (3mm) past the corner.

Step 4 Turn the board through 90° and repeat the procedure until all the sides are cut.

A selection of hand-held mount cutters and scalpel.

The piece of glass, used as a guide, positioned on the mount and the mount cutter.

The starting point for the cutter on one side of the mount.

Where to finish the cut.

If the centre will not come out when the cutter is removed, it is because the cuts have not joined at the corners. The remedy is simple: working on the finished side, take the scalpel and carefully extend the cuts into the corners until the centre is freed. Eventually, however, experience will enable you to judge where to start and finish the cuts without having to resort to the scalpel. Keep the centre piece; this can be taped to the reverse of the mount to help hold the artwork flat.

It is important to practise using the cutter; if you persevere, you will find it an ideal piece of equipment, very versatile and well suited to free-hand work.

I find the mountcutter blades need replacing after cutting approximately ten mounts; it is false economy to try to make them last longer as you will get a very raggedy edge to your bevels. Another cause of poor bevels is the cutting surface – this must be changed regularly to maintain precision.

If the cuts do not meet at the corners, gently extend the cuts with a scalpel until they meet.

The piece of board cut from the centre of the mount is taped to the back of the mount along one edge only; this ensures the artwork lays flat.

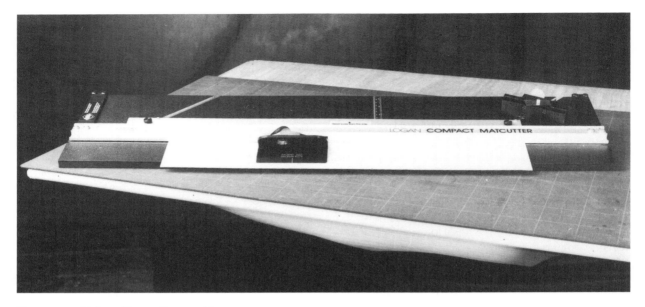

The more sophisticated Logan Compact Matcutter.

An Oval Mount

A photographic portrait can be greatly enhanced by
using an oval-shaped mount, particularly if it is of a
young girl or lady, as the gentle curve adds softness. It
is reasonably easy to cut an oval; a plate or dish can be
used as a template provided they are the required dimensions. If you try this method, proceed as follows:

An old photograph fitted in an oval mount.

Step 1   Place the template on the surface of the mount.
Step 2   Bring the bevel cutter into contact, and move it carefully around until the oval or circle is completed.

The main difficulty encountered in using this method is holding the template firm. It is slightly easier to use a straight 90° cut, and when confidence has been gained, progress to the more difficult bevel.

If you cannot find an object to use as a template, it is possible to draw an oval of the desired proportions, though try this on a scrap piece of card first, marking the reverse. Decide on the oval size, say 5 × 7in (130 × 180mm) and proceed thus:

Step 1   Draw a line 7in (180mm) long; in the centre of this,
Step 2   draw another line at 90° 5in (130mm) long so they form a cross.
Step 3   With your compasses, draw two 3½in (90mm) circles, which just touch, on the 7in (180mm) line.

Step 4   Now move the compasses to the end of the 5in (130mm) line and reset them until they just touch the tip of the 7in (180mm) line; transfer this measurement to the 5in (130mm) line and from this reference point re-adjust the compasses so that they just touch the circles and then draw the arc to complete one side of the oval.
Step 5   Repeat this step on the opposite end of the 5in (130mm) line, and you should have a perfect oval.

--- TIPS ---

By drawing your own ovals you can vary the proportions from the almost round to the very elongated, a shape often used by early photographers. As your confidence grows you may become more ambitious and cut a mount with two ovals; these *must* be marked accurately on the same plane, since any discrepancy will look awful. Imagine two ovals matching perfectly, but leaning to one side – they would never be acceptable.

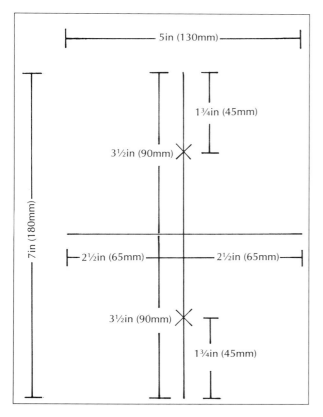

Drawing a 7 × 5in oval. (Not to scale.)

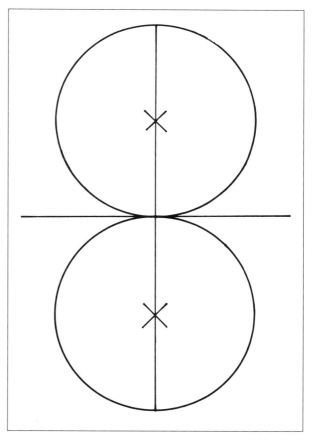

(b) Draw two 3in diameter circles above and below the central horizontal line.

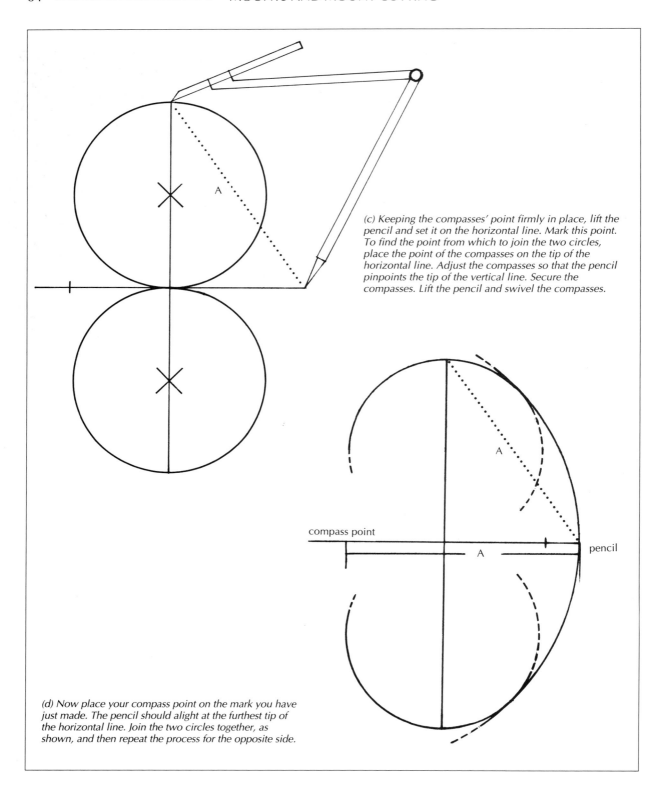

(c) Keeping the compasses' point firmly in place, lift the pencil and set it on the horizontal line. Mark this point. To find the point from which to join the two circles, place the point of the compasses on the tip of the horizontal line. Adjust the compasses so that the pencil pinpoints the tip of the vertical line. Secure the compasses. Lift the pencil and swivel the compasses.

compass point

pencil

(d) Now place your compass point on the mark you have just made. The pencil should alight at the furthest tip of the horizontal line. Join the two circles together, as shown, and then repeat the process for the opposite side.

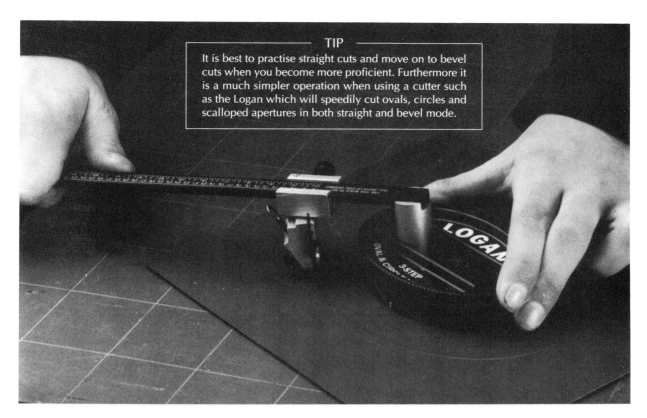

Cutting an oval mount with the Logan 3-way oval and circle mat-cutter.

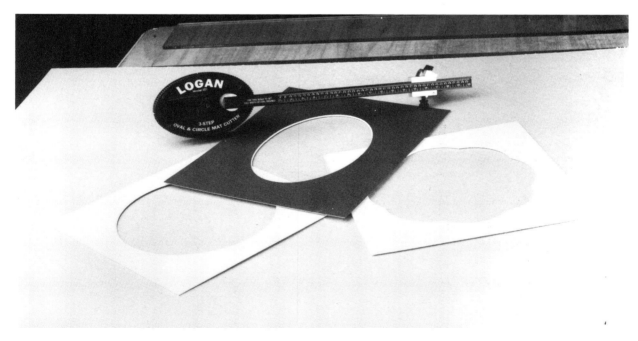

Samples of oval, circular and scalloped mounts.

Multiple Aperture Mounts

Multiple apertures are best marked out on the back of the mount board using a pencil grade such as 4H. Do not cut each window separately; it is better to fix the straight-edge and make all the cuts on that plane at one time, and to repeat this for each line to be sure the windows will be straight.

You may be asked to cut a mount for cigarette cards. These can be bought ready cut from some suppliers; they are mainly available die-cut to standard dimensions with a set number of apertures straight cut in mountboard. However, it is also possible to cut your own, following the same principles as for multiple aperture mounts. If you leave enough space, either ¼ or ½in (6 or 12mm), it is easier to cut bevel apertures. Alternatively, it is possible to cut this type of mount from thin card or cover paper (usually available from art shops). Use a scalpel to cut this material and hold it firmly as it has a tendency to wrinkle up if the blade is not very sharp.

Marking in pencil on the back of a mount board a multi-aperture mount.

Cutting the multi-aperture mount. (Note that all the cuts on the same plane are made without moving the glass straight-edge rather than cutting each aperture individually.)

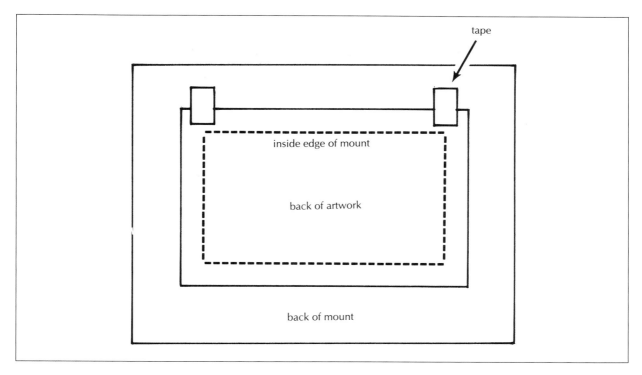

The correct way to tape the picture to the mount.

FIXING THE ARTWORK TO THE MOUNT

Taping

Never use masking tape or sellotape; neither of these is intended to be used for this purpose and they will dry out, allowing the artwork to slip, or worse still, the adhesive will migrate and penetrate the work. Once this happens it is impossible to remove and, being acid, it can destroy the area it has penetrated. For valuable pieces archival tape can be used: the adhesive is water soluble, it will not cause damage and it can be removed easily by soaking with distilled water then carefully peeling away. I always use distilled water, as it does not contain impurities and will not leave a stain when it has dried out. If the work has little value I would use brown gummed tape which is water soluble.

When mounting any artwork it is unnecessary to tape on all sides, in fact to do so can cause severe cockling – when the paper wants to expand as it absorbs moisture but cannot as the tape prevents any movement; so instead of lying flat, the paper develops unsightly waves. This can be overcome by taping at two points only, the ideal position being approximately 2in (50mm) from each corner along the top edge.

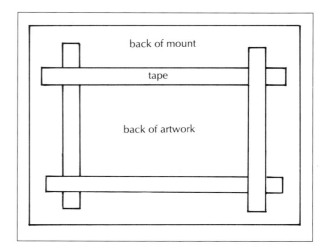

The incorrect way to tape the picture to the mount.

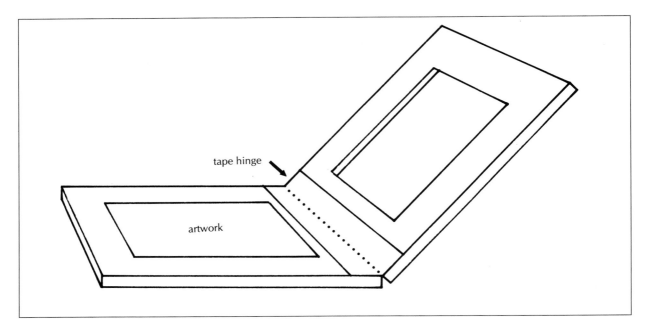

Making a hinge mount.

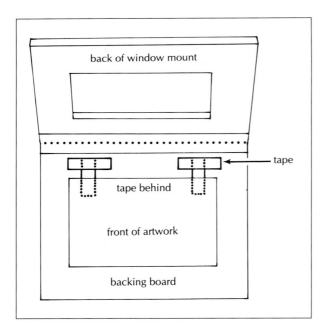

Taping artwork into the hinge mount.

Mounting a Valuable Piece

Acid-free conservation board provides the best environment. After calculating the overall size of mount board required, cut two identical pieces: on the first, mark and cut the window, then tape this to the remaining piece along the top edge so they hinge together. Raise the window and position the artwork on the base, carefully lining it up in the window. Next, fix a tape tab to the underside of the piece, then tape across the protruding tab fixing it firmly to the base board. This will allow the work to move with any atmospheric change and remain flat; it will also be easy to remove at any time in the future.

Floating

If all the piece is to show, this is called floating. Cut four pieces of tape and fold them over so they look like stamp hinges. Dampen them on one side, and fix to the reverse side of the artwork, making sure they are invisible when viewing the piece. Then dampen the other side of each hinge and place them on the mount, making sure they are correctly positioned. Place a weight on top to hold the artwork flat until the adhesive paper has dried.

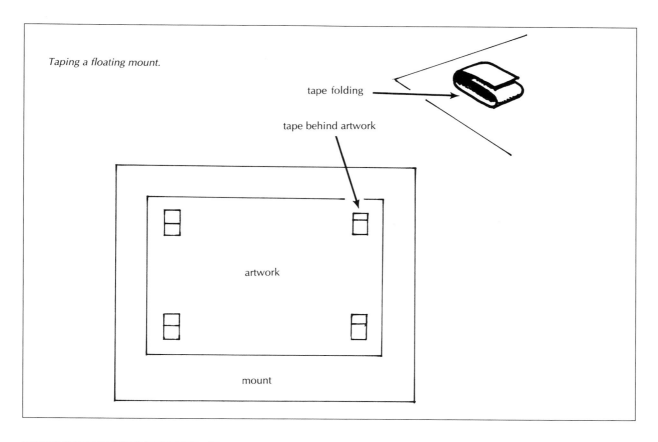

Taping a floating mount.

tape folding

tape behind artwork

artwork

mount

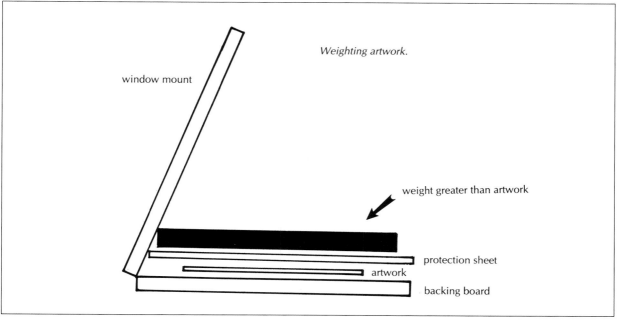

Weighting artwork.

window mount

weight greater than artwork

protection sheet

artwork

backing board

5

Mount Decoration

Having cut the mount we can add decoration, always bearing in mind that it is better to understate than to overdo, and that decoration should be compatible with the picture. As we have said, it is essential to choose colours which are complimentary to the picture and not intrusive.

LINING

We will start with simple lining which can be in pencil (ordinary, coloured or graphite), in coloured drawing inks, or the new range of pearlescent, watercolour or self-adhesive tape, or even felt pens. The first item we need is a template to mark the starting and finishing points at each corner: this is easily made from an off-cut of mount board about 4in (100mm) wide and 8in (200mm) long. Cut one end into a 45° angle and make marks along this diagonal at ⅛in (3mm) intervals; then

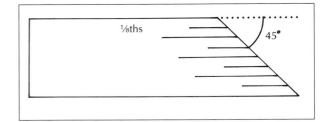

Corner marking template.

place the short side against the window, slide it towards the corner and, making sure it is square, prick with a pin or mark with a hard pencil along the diagonal where the lines will be drawn. Repeat this step at each corner. When drawing the lines with a pencil, I sometimes use a carpenter's pencil as this can give a line up to ¼in (6mm) wide; varying the pressure can make a more interesting effect.

Selection of lining pen, pencils, felt pens, brushes, acrylic and pearlescent inks used for lining mounts.

Using the homemade lining gauge to mark the corners.

A thick-leaded carpenter's pencil being used to apply lines to a mount.

> ——————— TIP ———————
> When using inks, check the suitability of the medium on an off-cut, as some will bleed into the board surface giving an unsatisfactory line.

Lining with Inks

A lining or ruling pen is used when drawing lines in ink or watercolour: this is a pen which is capable of producing lines of various thicknesses by means of its adjustable points. It is best to load the medium with a brush, gently wiping it against the nib; if you dip it into an ink pot the edges must be wiped before using it. Turn your ruler upside-down when drawing lines; this creates space between it and the mount and prevents the line dragging. You should load the pen with enough ink to draw a complete line, as it is not possible to stop and restart without showing the join.

The completed mount lines. Note the varying tones achieved by altering the pressure on the pencil, also the corner variations.

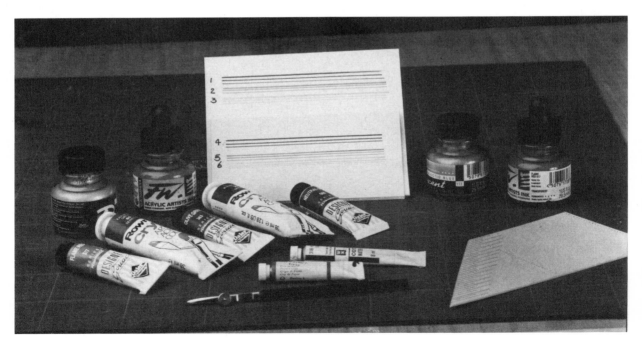

Test lines on mount board to check for the ink bleeding along with various mediums for wash lines.

Load the lining pen with a paintbrush rather than dipping the pen into the medium.

When ruling a line, this is the correct way to have the straight-edge.

A mount showing the correct spacing of the wash lines prior to adding the colour.

When preparing colours for lining with either ink or water, it is best to thin the medium as we want the colours muted rather than strong. Allow plenty of time so they are completely dry before attempting to add a wash.

Applying a Wash Line

Make sure everything is ready before attempting to add a wash line. Colours should be pale, well mixed and quite thin, as it is better to build the colour in several thin coats than to apply one thick one. Before starting the wash, dampen the area between the lines to which it will be applied with clean water; this will assist the colour to flow evenly and will prevent it drying out and leaving tide marks. Then, using a flat brush the width of the wash line, apply the colour: starting from a corner,

Applying water between the lines so the colour will flow freely.

Colour being applied: build up the colour with several thin coats rather than thick ones.

The completed mount.

work quickly round; have some cotton wool ready to mop up any excess colour – if it runs over the lines slightly, it is better to let it dry and then remove it with a sharp scalpel, or some very fine sandpaper. You will need a great deal of practice to become proficient at applying wash lines because it is very difficult to apply the colour evenly; but persevere – you will not regret it!

———————————— TIP ————————————
On the subject of lining, try adding small embellishments in the corners, nothing too ornate; I have illustrated some that are useful when mounting old photographs or art deco prints.

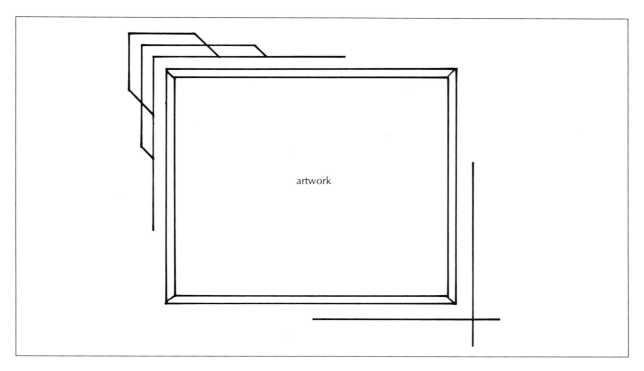

Embellishing a mount: four examples.

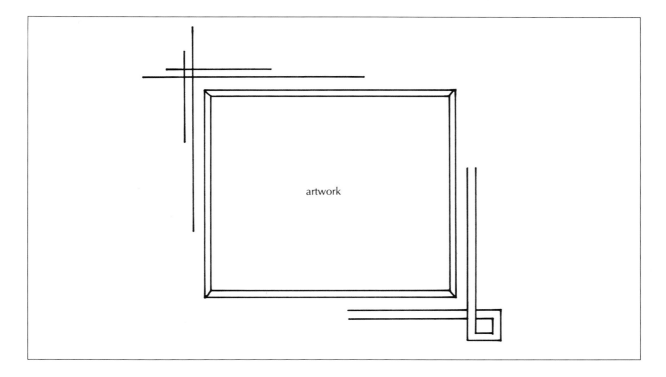

Self-adhesive tape which can be used for lining mounts.

Lining with Self-Adhesive Tape

Self-adhesive tape is available in several widths and finishes and is very easy to apply. The corner joints look better when mitred: take each piece just past the corner, then using a steel ruler as a guide, cut both pieces at the same time with a scalpel to ensure a perfect fit. Gold tape is particularly useful on boards with a porous surface that will not take ink; white tape is useful when lining on black board, as white ink soaks into the surface and appears a dirty grey. Alternatively the surface of the board can actually be removed to reveal the white core, cutting two parallel lines carefully with your scalpel and removing the centre.

Another variation on this theme is to cut thin strips of decorated paper and paste these carefully around the mount aperture; do make sure they are co-ordinated with the mounted subject, however.

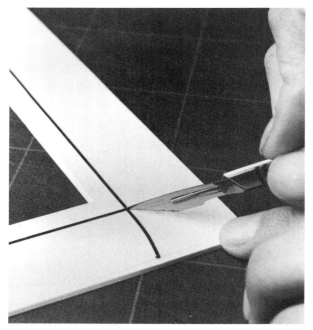

Finishing the corners with a mitre cut.

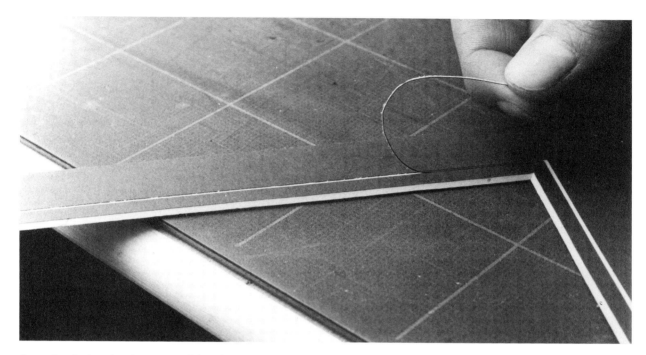

Removing the board surface to reveal the white core.

CUTTING OUT A DECORATIVE MOTIF

Another way of decorating a mount is to cut out a motif in the top board of a double mount allowing the lower board to show through. This can be very effective, particularly if the boards are contrasting colours, although it still works well when the boards are the same colour.

Be adventurous with your motifs. For example, if you are making a mount to accompany a picture of fruit, cut out the shapes of various fruits, perhaps with a different fruit in each corner. Remember to make the designs in the bottom corners larger than the ones in the top corners or the end result will be unbalanced. Another possibility is to create a design in the bottom edge only; I have seen intricate lattice work used to good effect (although it must have taken a considerable time to mark out and cut!)

Choose colours with care; you can create interest by using a different colour insert in the lower mount. To achieve this effect, mark the position of the motif accurately on the bottom mount, then cut the colour insert slightly larger than the motif. Mark the size of the insert on the bottom board and cut it out with a scalpel, then tape the insert in place. Be wary of creating too great a colour contrast – subtlety and discretion give the best results.

Top board of a double mount with a design cut into it revealing the contrasting colour of the lower board.

USING DECORATIVE PAPER

After cutting the window, the board can be covered with a decorative paper: medium- or lightweight paper is preferable as it is easier to manipulate around the edges and make a neat finish. Remember to choose a board colour compatible with the covering you are using as it could show through a thin paper; a white or an off-white board can give an attractive luminance to the covering so is always a safe choice. A bevel-cut mount works best, although you may use a straight-cut one.

Carry out the paper-covering process as follows:

Step 1 The paper must first be trimmed to be 1in (25mm) larger than the overall size of the mount.

Step 2 The next stage is gluing, for which use a suitable paper paste: I find the ready-mixed, heavy-duty wallpaper and hessian paste very good, as it can be thinned with water and it also contains a fungicide.

Apply a thin coat to the board surface, making sure it is spread evenly.

Step 3 Position the paper over the mount, making sure any pattern is running parallel with the edges. Cover with a piece of scrap paper and smooth down, either with a soft cloth or a roller.

Step 4 Remove any bubbles, then turn the mount over and wipe away all excess adhesive which has been squeezed around the edges.

Step 5 Turn face up, and place under even pressure. A barrier such as a piece of clean greaseproof paper should be put between the mount and any weight.

Step 6 Once dry, the outer edges can be finished, so place the mount face down on a clean surface and make a diagonal cut across each corner.

Step 7 Apply paste to the back of the board, one side at a time, and then carefully fold the paper round the edge, making sure it is stretched tightly; the diagonal cut will help in forming a neat mitre at each corner.

Steel rule, adhesive, scalpel, mount and cover paper for mount decoration.

Applying adhesive to the mount surface.

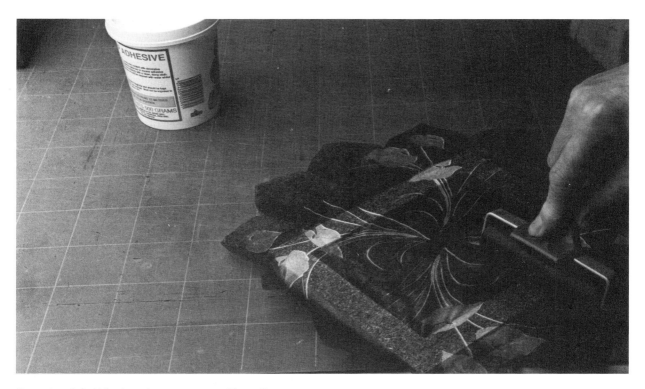

Removing air bubbles from the cover paper with a roller.

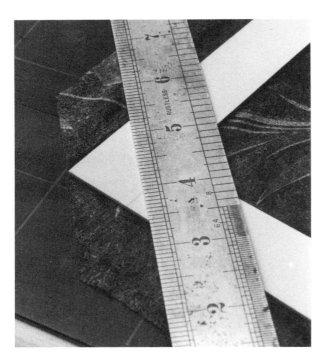

Diagonal corner cut prior to folding the decorative paper on to the mount.

Step 8   With the board face down, the next step is to cut out the aperture; remember that ½in (12mm) of paper must be allowed all round the aperture to fold round the back. With a scalpel or very sharp knife, carefully mitre right into the corners.

Step 9   Then apply the paste and press down. Place under even pressure as before, and leave to dry.

The same processes are used when covering boards with an oval or circular aperture, though with these when finishing the window, make cuts outwards from the bevel edge at approximately ½in (12mm) intervals; this will enable a neat edge to be achieved. Paste down and weight until dry.

The finished decorated mount.

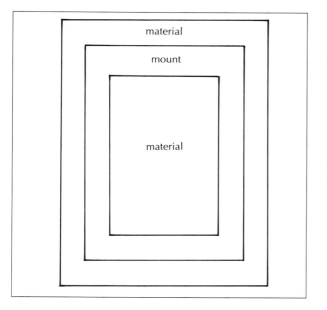

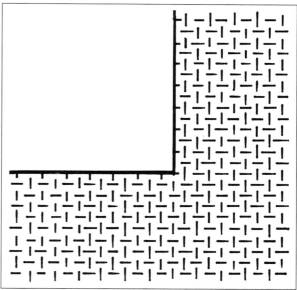

Edge of mount, with material showing direction of weave.

USING DECORATIVE MATERIAL

Similar techniques are used when covering a mount with material:

Step 1 Follow the same principles regarding sizes.
Step 2 Apply a thin coat of PVA adhesive to the board and allow to dry.
Step 3 Carefully position the material over the mount, lining up the weave so it is parallel to the board edges, then place a piece of scrap paper over and, making sure there are no wrinkles, iron it over; the heat from the iron reactivates the adhesive.
Step 4 Keep it weighted evenly until the mount has cooled, then trim and finish as before.

A further variation is to place a piece of thin foam under the covering; this gives a padded effect.

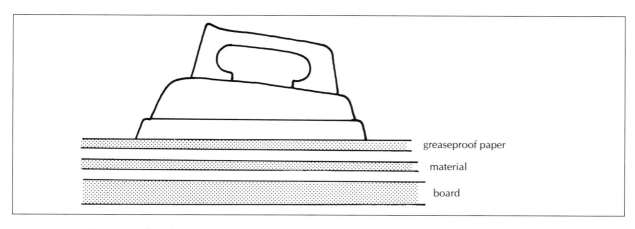

Activating the adhesive with heat from an electric iron.

EMBOSSING

Embossing is yet another way of decorating a mount. Using a small screwdriver with a highly polished finish, simple lines can be impressed into the board surface. The screwdriver must be polished because if it is left with a rough edge this will damage the board surface. I polish mine with metal polish and only use it for embossing. Several gentle passes create better lines. Move around the mount equally rather than embossing one side at a time. More complex designs are possible by making a pattern piece from card – harder material can actually cut the surface of the board – and placing this under pressure for several hours. The procedure for making a pattern can be time-consuming, and requires patience plus accurate cutting. Proceed as follows:

Step 1   Start by drawing the design full size on tracing paper; in the example I am creating a pattern of triangles ¼in (6mm) away from the window, and 1in (25mm) from base to apex. The window measures 8 × 10in (203 × 254mm), and the first step is to draw the aperture and the ¼in (6mm) border line around it.

Step 2   Draw the outer limit 1in (25mm) wide, then mark the centre point of each side.

Step 3   Starting at the centre of the top of the mount, map out the triangles lightly until equal spacing is achieved; the bottom (the opposite side) can be copied from this. Then move to each side and repeat the procedure.

Step 4   Cut from a scrap piece the number of triangles required, and glue them onto the tracing paper.

Step 5   When they are completely dry, place the pattern face down on top of the mount which should have the window cut out ready. You will be able to position the pattern accurately as the mount will be visible through the tracing paper.

Step 6   When you are satisfied with the positioning, place a piece of plywood or something similar on top and weight evenly with books. Leave for twenty-four hours, although this time may vary according to the type of board used; it is as well to carry out some trials to determine the time required to achieve best effect. When the pattern is removed, you will have a mount with your own distinct embossed design.

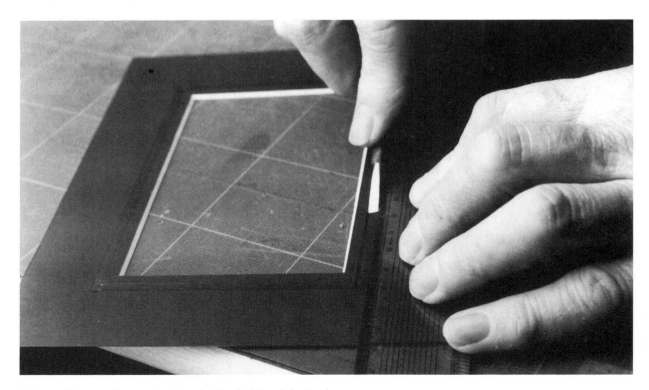

Embossed line round a mount achieved with a highly polished tool.

Cutting out triangles from scrap mountboard.

The design is started by gluing the triangles in each corner.

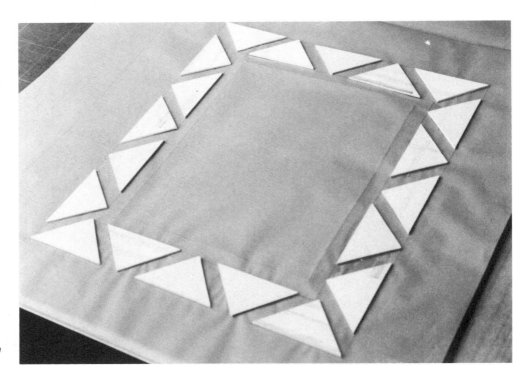

The completed design ready for the press.

The finished embossed mount with the photograph fitted.

A very effective way of mounting an old photograph is to paste it to a piece of watercolour paper and, when it is dry, to paint a line with distilled water approximately ¼in (6mm) away from the print, using a small paint brush. Allow the water to soak into the paper, then gently pull the paper apart leaving an attractive deckled edge. Paste the watercolour paper onto a darker piece of mount board, and you will have created an attractive variation.

The completed deckled edge watercolour paper, photograph and mount.

6

Mouldings

There are many hundreds of ready-made mouldings available, with costs ranging from a few pence to over a hundred pounds per foot, and finishes varying from varnished wood to the elaborately carved and gilded and the highly decorative. Nevertheless they all have their place in the framer's repertoire, and in this chapter we will look at some suggested uses for them, bearing in mind there are no hard and fast rules regarding their use. There are, however, certain traditional uses, and the framer should be aware of these.

CHOOSING A MOULDING

Oils and acrylics painted on canvas or board are usually framed without glass, as the finished painting is given a coat of varnish which provides the protection needed; being placed behind glass would not allow the impasto techniques to be fully shown off. Large mouldings suit oils and acrylics, although it is important al-

ways to take the picture to be framed with you when selecting the moulding. Try high backed and reverse samples against the picture: see how the eye is held in the frame by a high back, and led gently in by a reverse moulding. Try the effect of a light gold frame on a portrait, and compare this with a plain varnished wood; or choose between a heavy ornate gold moulding or a dark-stained wood when framing a landscape scene. Try inserting a gold or neutral painted slip between the picture and the frame to act as a sight line or a visual separation; be aware of colour contrasts and co-ordinations; and remember that when all is said and done, there are no hard and fast rules, only your own personal preferences.

Mouldings for Watercolours

Watercolours are traditionally framed with small mouldings and large mounts. The moulding finishes can range from gold, which suits the majority, to the contemporary

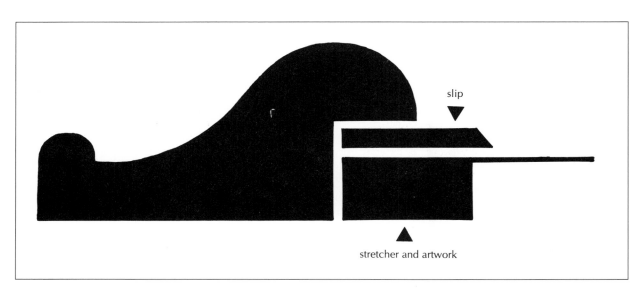

Moulding with a 'slip'.

High back moulding.

Reverse moulding.

Spoon moulding.

Hockey-stick moulding.

Cushion moulding.

pastel coloured. Care is needed if choosing pastel colours, however, as a bland, uninteresting effect can result if everything is too co-ordinated. Do not be afraid to put a small picture in a 4 or 6in (100 or 150mm) mount as this will give the opportunity to add wash lines and can be very effective.

TIP

The very delicately decorated mouldings available today are ideal for some of the modern watercolours. Choose carefully, and the moulding will help enhance the feeling of peace and tranquillity intended by the artist; similarly bright colours can match the freedom and vibrancy found in a child's painting.

Frames for Modern Prints

Modern prints by artists such as Picasso look very good when framed in stark metal-finish mouldings, depending on the colours and subject matter of the picture. Look at the matt chrome or gold finishes: try contrasting a warm gold with a cool print, or cold chrome with a warm print. Some of the small airbrushed prints can be shown at their best when framed in a small cushion moulding without a mount. Bright colours, too, can be very effective; however, use black selectively as it can give a heavy, sombre feel.

Framing Traditional Prints and Maps

Traditional prints and antiquarian maps are often framed in a Hogarth moulding: this is black with a gold sight line and decoration, and the back edge is traditionally grooved; I believe this was to hold a cord in place, used to keep the joints tight while they were setting.

Certificates

Certificates can look good framed in small glossy black moulding with a gold sight edge. Many have the coloured crest or logo of the issuing body, and this can be picked up in the choice of mount colour. Bright reds and blues are very effective: this is an instance when the mount is used to attract the eye to the certificate, which on its own would not draw the attention in the way a picture would; the bright colours serve this purpose.

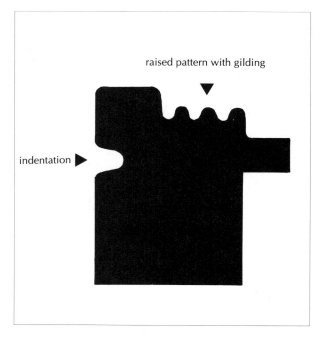

raised pattern with gilding

indentation

Hogarth moulding.

Frames for Tapestries

Tapestries need a moulding with a deep rebate to allow the stretcher to be as flush as possible with the back edge of the frame. This also applies to découpage framing where the artwork is spaced from the glass by means of an inner or box frame. Walnut and pine mouldings are popular choices of finish for tapestries, whilst découpage work suits many types of moulding, depending on the subject and colour of the artwork. It really is essential that the subject to be framed is in front of you when you are choosing the moulding.

Frames for Embroideries and Needlepoints

Small embroideries and needlepoints can be framed in most small gold or cushion mouldings. The ½in (12mm) cushions are available in many colours and interesting effects can be created by choosing contrasting moulding and mount combinations. Try using a pale mount and a strong moulding of the same hue, say green, if it complements the subject; note how the strong moulding holds in the eye, but if this colour co-ordination were to be reversed the dominant feature would be the mount – which is not the desired effect.

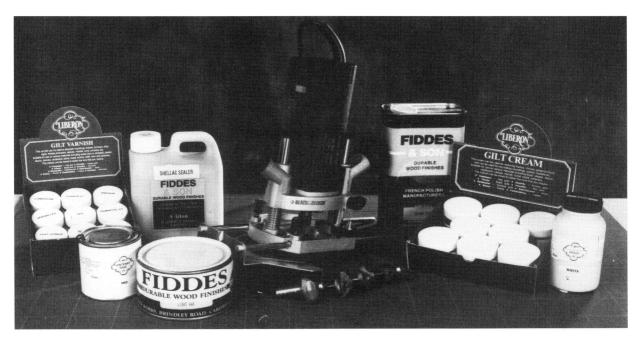

Tools and equipment needed to shape and finish your own moulding.

Framing Important Documents

A neutral moulding is best used to frame important documents. The interest in these is historical rather than artistic and the object of framing this type of work is firstly to preserve them, with display of secondary importance. With the emphasis on preservation the choice of mount is critical and calls for an acid free or museum board hinge mount as described on page 68.

PRODUCING YOUR OWN MOULDINGS

In this section we will explore some ideas on making and applying various finishes to mouldings of our own design and manufacture.

Any moulding is best made in one length, to ensure good matching when the mitres are made. Examine the piece carefully and be sure to select a length which is straight and warp free; check also for knots and avoid if possible. Consider how the moulding will be finished – if it is to be painted or gilded the grain pattern is less important than it would be for a polished finish.

TOOLS

- Pencil
- Rule
- Router with various cutters
- PVA woodworking adhesive
- A selection of wood stains
- Sealers and polishes
- Brushes
- 0000 gauge wire wool

Choice of Wood

When making your own mouldings the choice of wood is crucial. The qualities required are that the wood must be stable – that is, not prone to warping or splitting – and that it has an attractive grain; this is essential if a stained or polished finish is desired. It must also be machinable. Timbers which have these qualities include ash, ramin, obeche, jelutong, mahogany and oak.

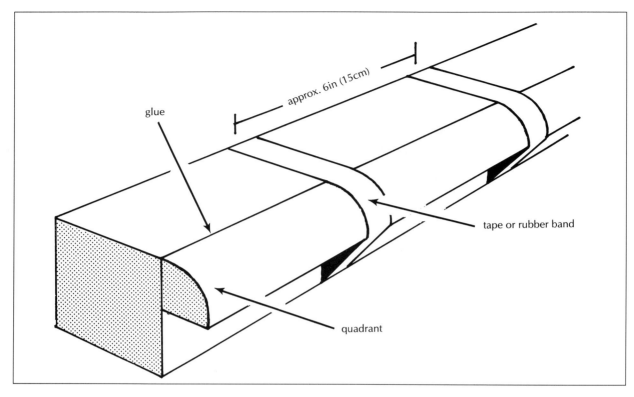

The most basic moulding.

A Basic Moulding

The most basic moulding we can manufacture is made using two pieces of timber; as ramin is readily available and easy to work, it is ideal to start with. The main piece is 1in (25mm) square, with a piece of ½in (12mm) quadrant beading glued to it, forming the rebate; it should be held in place with rubber bands or masking tape until the glue is set. Make sure that no adhesive finds its way onto the surface, as this will form a water-resistant barrier and thus prevent any stain we may wish to apply from penetrating the wood, giving a blotchy, unattractive finish. When the adhesive is dry, lightly rub down the moulding with abrasive paper, firstly with 240 (medium) grit and finishing with 500 (fine) grit.

Staining and Polishing

It is advisable to carry out any staining or polishing procedures before mitring and jointing as it is much easier to brush-stain a straight length; nor are there any corners where stain can collect giving a heavy concentrated colour. Once the stain has dried it will need a coat of sealer, which must be rubbed down using 0000 wire wool. Wax polish can be applied next: rub it in well using the wire wool, and buff with a soft cloth. The moulding is now ready for mitring and assembling in the usual way.

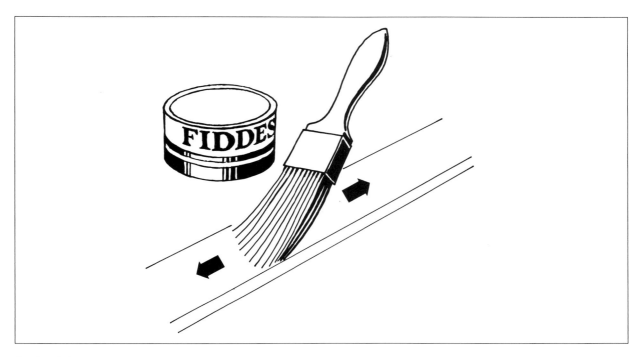

Brush staining.

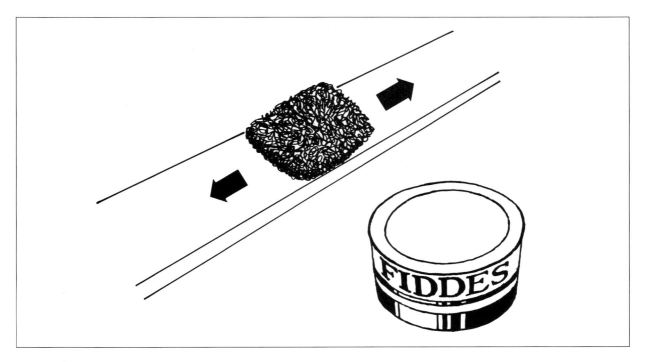

Polish and wire wool.

Mouldings Using a Router

First have a clear idea of the design you are going to create. Then draw some rough sketches to help you decide on the proportions, always bearing in mind the finished frame and the picture to be sure they will be compatible. It is usual to rout a single length of wood and then mitre it to the required lengths, so be generous with your measurements to make certain you have enough wood. The wood must be clamped firmly at each end before starting the routing – remember to allow extra for this purpose. If you are creating a design where the routing stops before the corner instead of continuing round it, then the wood must be mitred to length first and then the design marked out and carefully routed.

More elaborate mouldings can be manufactured using a router and a selection of cutters; these vary from straight-shanked, used to form the rebate; domed cutters which will make fluted cuts; to cutters which will round off the corners giving a smooth, curvy shape. The moulding can then be sealed with acrylic primer, and finished off by rubbing down.

Router fitted with straight cutter used to form the rebate.

A selection of router cutters.

A router forming a rounded corner.

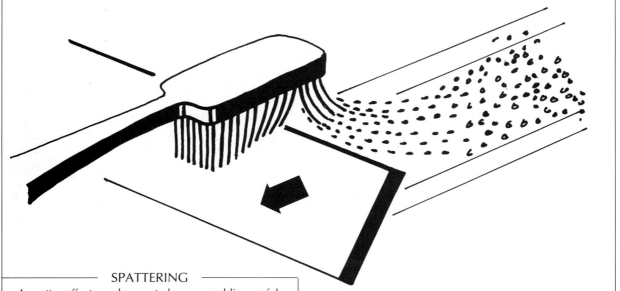

SPATTERING

A spatter effect can be created on a moulding as follows: first, give it a coat of acrylic primer, then apply a base coat; when that is dry, dip a toothbrush into a second colour, which can either contrast with or match the base coat. Hold it two or three inches from the moulding, then draw an off-cut of mount board across the bristles, moving it towards you; this will create random speckles. When dry, these can be given a coat of clear acrylic varnish, glossy or matt, whichever you decide. Experiment by spattering onto a wet or part-dried base coat and allowing the two applications to blend – though always test on a scrap of moulding before commencing work on the real thing.

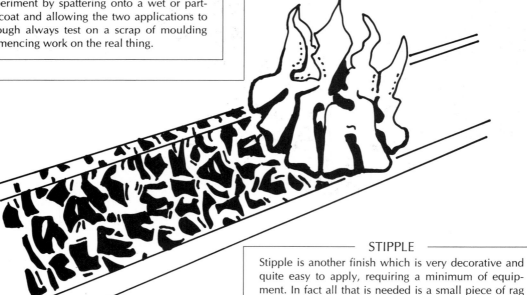

STIPPLE

Stipple is another finish which is very decorative and quite easy to apply, requiring a minimum of equipment. In fact all that is needed is a small piece of rag rolled into a sausage shape; dip this into paint, then roll it gently over the moulding surface, creating a random pattern. This is very effective when applied over a base colour.

Carving Mouldings

An alternative to routing is to carve your frames. Choose an easy-to-work wood such as lime, sycamore, or a good quality pine from temperate climate zones; these woods are sustainable. If tropical woods are to be used, types such as lauan, meranti or obeche will be found to be suitable. The carved frame could then be gilded.

Carving on a frame can be continuous. In this case the frame must be assembled first, then the design marked out and carved. This method will give a carving that flows round each corner, matching perfectly. Each length of moulding could be carved before assembly with the same design in a central position. You may wish to start with a very simple design carved only in the bottom rail. Do not attempt anything too ambitious in the beginning; the simple pattern illustrated was carved with two chisels, a 60 degrees V tool no. 39 was used to create the curves and a ¼in (6mm) no. 9 gouge for the central design. In this case the moulding was stained Jacobean oak before carving commenced

so the design is more prominent. Keep your carving simple to begin with and as your skills and confidence grow, move on to more elaborate designs. You can always practise on offcuts before attempting the real thing.

Flowing, sweeping designs will suit traditional landscape and portrait pictures; try angular or geometric designs for contemporary and abstract painting.

A router will remove large areas of wood more speedily than a mallet and wood chisel; this process is termed 'roughing out', and is carried out after the design has been marked out on the assembled frame and the outline chased round with a V tool. Make sure you wear eye protection (either safety glasses or a face mask, whichever you find most comfortable) and ensure that the frame is held securely before beginning roughing out. The frame can then have the design worked with the mallet and wood chisels. Remove the wood in small bites to create texture and then sand with fine paper before finishing with either a wax polish or varnish, matt, semi-gloss or gloss according to personal preference.

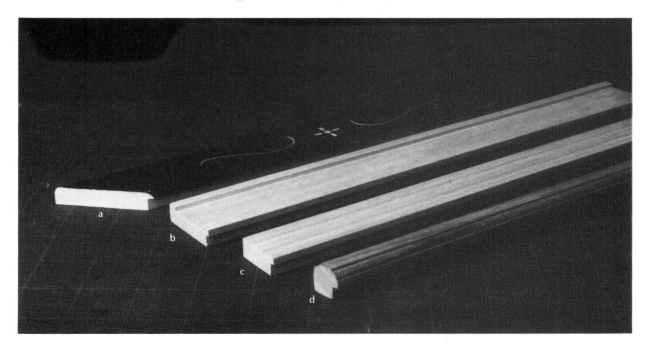

Examples of mouldings. (a) After forming the rebate the front and rear edges were rounded and the piece was stained before the simple design was carved using a 60 degrees V tool no. 39 and a ¼in (6mm) gouge. (b) The centre of this piece was removed by routing followed by careful sanding as preparation for the application of gesso. (c) This example has had two flutes routed using a ¼in (6mm) domed tool. (d) This is a piece of oak which, after the rebate was formed, had front and rear edges rounded to leave a high ridge in the centre before applying a Fontenay base and then gilding.

This example of a corner cut from a length of bought moulding shows the difficulty of obtaining a perfect pattern match when turning the corner. This is not a problem if you carve the design yourself, but do not attempt anything too ambitious to start with.

The tools used to produce the design described in the photograph on page 97.

A selection of abrasive papers used in preparing mouldings prior to the application of Fontenay Base.

GILDING

Preparing the Wood

Successful gilding needs careful preparation of the wood. The untreated timber will require sanding with various grades of abrasive paper starting with a 150 grit (coarse), moving on to 240 grit (medium), and finishing with 500 (fine) grit.

Fontenay Base

Once the wood has been sanded and any blemishes eradicated, a suitable foundation for the gilt has to be formed. This is done by applying a succession of coats of 'Fontenay Base' which has the consistency of thin cream. Wood for fully fledged gold-leaf gilding is prepared with a plaster-like substance called 'gesso'; for gilt varnish work Fontenay Base is more usually employed, as it is a simple preparation to apply to the

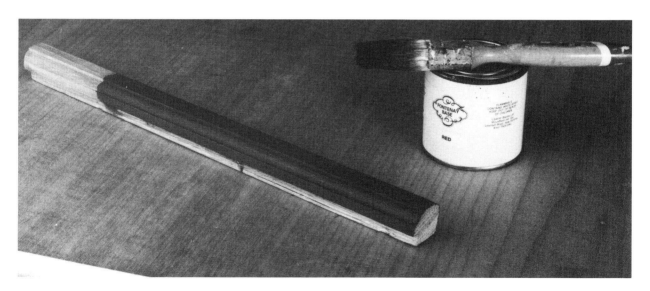

A short length of moulding which has been given two coats of Fontenay Base. The grain has started to fill and we are on the way to a very smooth finish. Note the untreated section left to make handling easier.

This sample piece has been given a coat of gilt varnish on the left and gilt cream on the right. I applied the varnish with a brush and the cream with my finger.

wood. The object is to fill the grain and create a smooth, matt surface. Usually four or five coats of Fontenay Base will need to be applied. Sand each coat thoroughly with fine-grade abrasive paper.

Fontenay Base is available in three basic colours: red, black and yellow. Choice will depend on the final finish required and some experimentation may be necessary. For regular gilt, yellow is best; for bronze, use the red; and for pewter, use the black – or the colours can be mixed as necessary.

Gilt Varnish

There is a wide range of gilt varnish colours. Most have attractive traditional names: for example, Chantilly is a bright nineteenth-century gold; Trianon is orange gold; and Versailles is a red-based gold.

I have distressed this sample to give it an antique feel by rubbing back with a piece of fine abrasive paper; try to do this in a random fashion for a realistic effect.

DISTRESSING GILT

A gilt finish can be given an 'aged' look by rubbing back some of the varnish until the base coat shows through; the more random the fashion in which this is done the more authentic a finish will be achieved. This process is called 'distressing'.

USING GESSO

To create a very different and attractive finish, ready-made gesso can be used, applied in two coats. Allow the first one to dry, then apply the second one and inscribe a pattern in the surface before it dries; when it is dry, colouring can commence. Apply a base coat of acrylic paint and allow it to dry thoroughly. Next, mix a very dilute coat and apply it so the base coat shows through a translucent layer. Finally apply a coat of acrylic varnish for protection, and you have created a unique finish. Experiment with different colour combinations: for example, use a light base coat and apply a darker top coat; before it is completely dry, wipe off the colour from the high spots, leaving the darker colour to remain in the recesses.

The only limit to applying a finish is your imagination.

This moulding has had its first coat of gesso.

The gesso has been inscribed using a small screwdriver.

A thin coat of light grey acrylic paint has been applied and allowed to dry.

A coat of black acrylic paint has been applied over the base coat and rubbed off the high points allowing the lighter base coat to show through. This is now ready for a finishing coat of acrylic varnish.

7

Framing Needlework and Embroidery

STRETCHING TAPESTRY

There are many ways of stretching tapestries; however, I shall describe just the three that I have used. Before we start we need to be certain the work is square, and if it is not, whether or not we will be able to correct any discrepancies. A visual check will tell how far out of square the item is, and a gentle tug diagonally in both directions will give some idea of the tension needed to correct it. The type of canvas the tapestry has been worked on plays a large part in the next process: if it is the flexible type, corrections of up to 2in (50mm) can be made when stretching on the frame, but with anything greater than this, or if the work is on the stiffer type of canvas, it is advisable to make the correction before stretching.

Squaring Tapestry

I have a piece of white melamine I keep for the purpose of bringing tapestries square; it is 4 × 2ft (1,200 × 600mm), and is the best material for this purpose because the facing is sealed and waterproof so no colour transfers onto the tapestry.

Step 1 The first step is to place the work face down on the melamine and pin a corner.

Step 2 Then put tension along the longest edge and

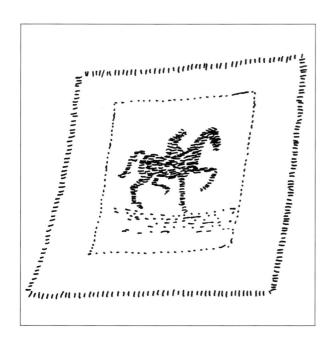

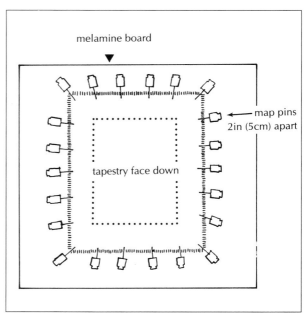

Pinning a tapestry square. (a) Tapestry before mounting. (b) Pin tapestry face down and spray with distilled water.

pin at 2in (50mm) intervals, keeping it as straight as possible.

Step 3 Next pin a short side as before, making sure the corner is at 90°; complete the pinning on the other sides, again making certain that all the corners are right angles.

Step 4 Lightly spray the back of the tapestry with distilled water, and gently rub it into the fibres. Do not soak the back or use anything but distilled water: this will ensure that the colours in the wools do not run or stains appear – which would happen if tap water were used.

Step 5 Leave overnight to dry: next day when you release the work it should be a true square or rectangle.

Stretching: Method One

The first method of stretching the tapestry is the traditional way:

Step 1 Cut a piece of stiff board, such as framer's

backing, approximately ⅛in (3mm) larger than the piece to be stretched; that is to say, if the piece is 12 × 10in (300 × 254mm) the board size will be 12⅛ × 10⅛in (303 × 257mm). The correct way to assess the size of any material to be stretched is to hold each side straight against a rule without any tension; check all four sides, and then add ⅛in (3mm) to the shortest length and the same amount to the shortest width. Tapestries are often unequal in shape, particularly if worked by a beginner or freehand (not on a frame).

Step 2 Fold the two longest sides round the board, and with canvas thread sew in a zig-zag across the two sides, starting at the top and working your way in ½in (12mm) steps to the bottom, taking great care to ensure the work is square and the tension even.

Step 3 When this is satisfactory, finish off the thread, fold over the two short sides and repeat the operation.

Like most things, the actual work involved in this process takes much longer to carry out than to explain the

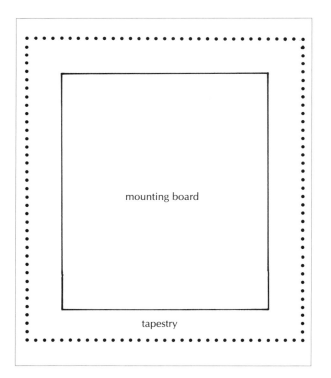

Lacing a tapestry over a board. (a) With the tapestry face down, place the mounting board centrally over the back of it. (b) Starting with the longer sides, lace the edges together, taking care to ensure even tension. (c) Lace the shorter sides together.

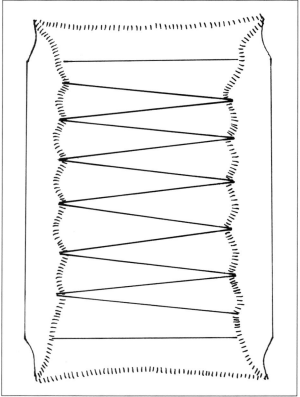

(b)

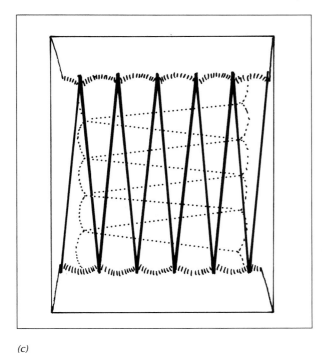

(c)

technique, and requires much patience. The advantages of this method are the ease with which the tapestry can be removed for cleaning, and the fact that no damage is done by way of putting in tacks or staples. The disadvantage is the length of time it takes to complete.

Method Two

Step 1   Construct a frame of planed timber 2 × ½in (50 × 12mm), making it ¼in (6mm) larger than the work all round. If the work is longer than 2ft (600mm), it is advisable to fit a centre support midway between the two longer sides. Then plane the outer edge to take off the sharpness.

Step 2   Starting at any corner, tack or fire in staples along the edge for up to 2in (50mm) each side of the corner; then move in a clockwise direction to the next corner and, carefully picking out the same line of stitching, repeat the tacking.

Step 3   When all four corners are secured, tack along the longest sides, then the shorter; you will probably

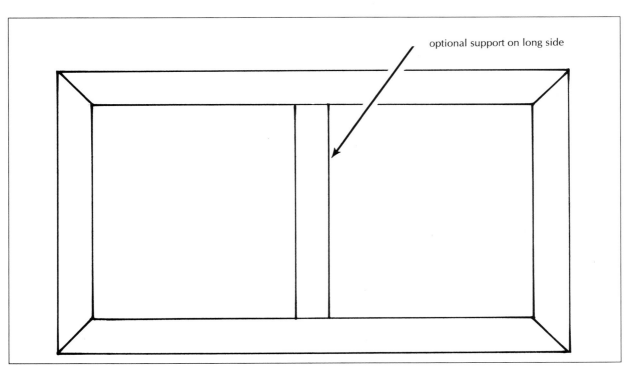

optional support on long side

Make a frame out of 2 × ½in timber.

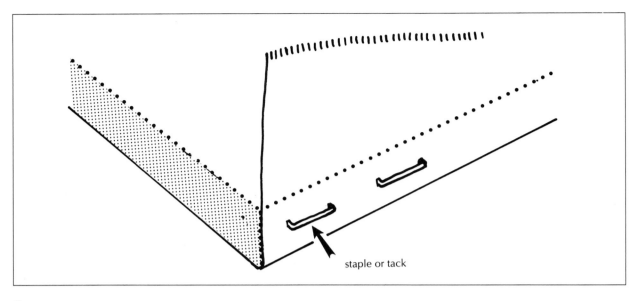

Corner.

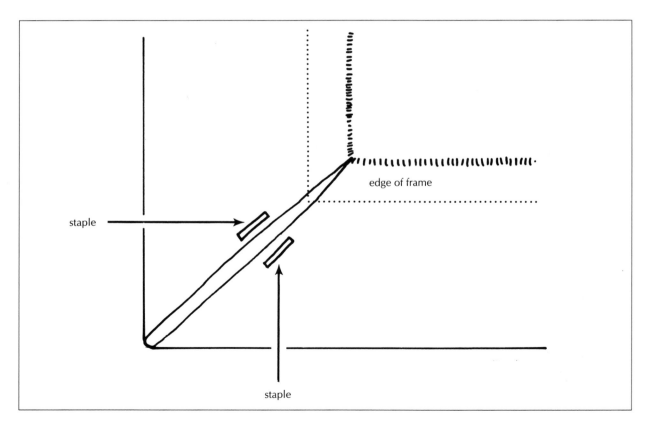

Finished corner fold.

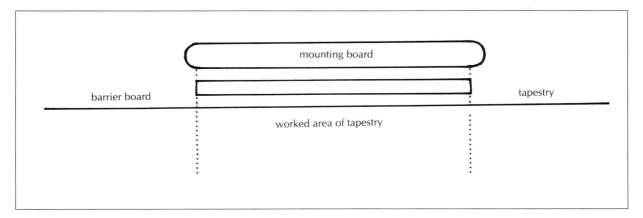

Position of barrier board. (Note the rounded edges of the mounting board.)

need tapestry pliers to do this, in order to save your fingers too much wear.

Step 4 Finish the back by tacking the excess material to the reverse of the frame, using hospital corners for neatness.

This is a very quick way to get a nicely tensioned, very square job, the only disadvantage being that the tacking and stapling leaves small holes in the canvas. In my opinion, however, this is not too great a price to pay.

Method Three

The third way needs several clothes pegs, both wood and plastic; it is the one I normally use.

Step 1 Cut a piece of ⅛in (3mm) hardboard, ⅛in (3mm) larger than the work; with a small plane, round all the edges so there is a smooth curve from the face to the reverse with no sharp corners which in time can damage the material. The hardboard must also have a protective layer between it and the material being stretched to reduce the possibility of discoloration arising from direct contact with the board; a good quality cartridge paper or, better still, barrier board is the answer.

Step 2 Place the piece face down on the work surface and position the board, with the barrier board in contact with the material, on top.

Step 3 Starting at a corner, fold the material round the hardboard and secure it with a wooden peg. Work

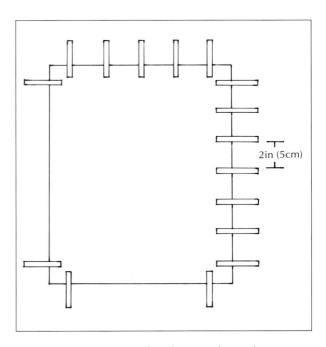

Pegging. Secure one corner first, then complete each side in rotation, leaving 2in (5cm) between pegs.

your way round the edges pegging roughly every 2in (50mm).

Step 4 When it is pegged all round, run a thin line of PVA adhesive on to the hardboard where the canvas edge reaches and press it into contact; but take care not to let the adhesive touch any wooden peg – if contact is made, substitute the peg for a plastic one. As regards

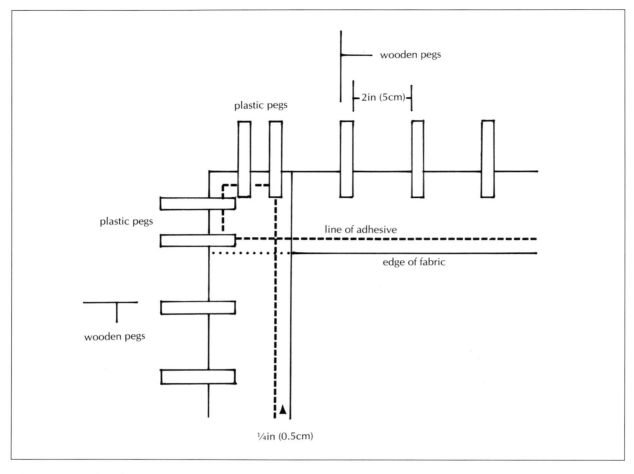

Gluing tapestry to board.

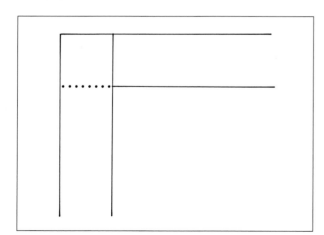

The finished corner, viewed from the back.

the corners, follow the illustration showing the correct method.

Step 5 After all the edges have been stuck down, leave overnight. The following day remove the pegs.

Thus you will have a neatly stretched tapestry, which furthermore can be removed by dampening the adhesive with warm water, leaving it completely undamaged.

┌─────────────── CAUTION ───────────────┐

Needlepoints are usually worked on a backing with clearly visible lines, so make sure these run parallel with the edge of the mount; if they do not, keep trying until they do, as nothing looks worse than straight lines running out of true.

SMALL PIECES, NEEDLEWORK AND EMBROIDERY

These are usually framed with a mount. The material used does not lend itself to the same stretching techniques as tapestries as there is not so much give in it, so they need just a very light tensioning. This is achieved by taping them to the mount. Use the sort of brown gummed tape which needs activating with water, because at a later date it can be removed easily by gently soaking the back. Masking tape will dry out and lose all its adhesion, allowing the piece to move; also the adhesive will migrate from its backing and eat into the fabric, and this will cause irreparable damage because once it gets into a surface it is impossible to remove. If your needlework is not being mounted, fold it round a piece of board taking care the board colour will not show through; if it does, use a piece of white board, and tape it to the back using the same gummed tape.

Samplers

Modern samplers can be treated in the same way as needlework and embroideries, but when working with old pieces – I have framed several over a hundred years old – they need to be handled with great care to avoid damage. Often they have been worked to the very edge of the base material, leaving no room to tension by any of the techniques described earlier. Besides, I like to show the complete piece on these occasions, and consider that the uneven edges add charm to the finished product. Use only conservation board with old pieces, to be sure they are in the safest environment you can give them.

Step 1 Using a compatible thread and a very sharp needle, catch the sampler through the back of the conservation board approximately every 2in (50mm) all the way round, making sure the stitches are not visible. Do not try to square up out-of-true edges, but leave them in their original shape; use only the lightest tension, just enough to prevent any sagging or wrinkling.
Step 2 Put a mount cut from conservation board round the fixed sampler to prevent contact with the glass, and you have a piece which will remain in the best condition possible.

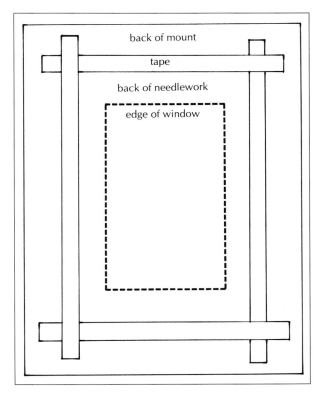

Taping needlework to a mount.

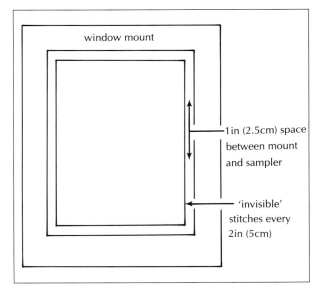

A stretched sampler mounted on conservation mount board.

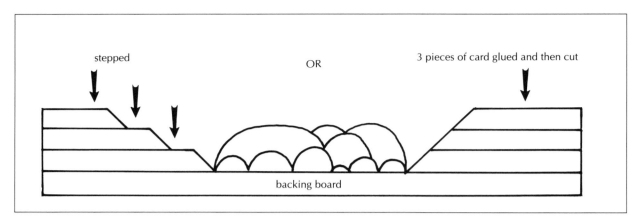

A triple mount, for work such as quilting. (Not to scale.)

QUILTING

Quilting presents a different set of problems to overcome, the main one being the depth of the work. This can be solved by using double or triple mounts. Alternatively a second frame, or box frame, can be fitted inside the main one; this can be stained, polished or painted to complement the quilting and the outer frame. Its main objective, however, is to keep the quilting out of contact with the glass.

TENSIONING AN OIL PAINTING

Occasionally we are presented with an unstretched oil painting on canvas, sometimes bought whilst its owners were on holiday abroad and usually rolled with the painted side inwards: this may seem to give protection to the picture, but it is in fact the wrong way to treat painted canvas, which should be rolled paint outwards; this slightly stretches the paint, whereas rolling it inwards compresses the paint and can cause it to crack when unrolled. Always inspect carefully any painting presented to you in this way, and point out any damage; if you omit to do this you may be wrongly accused of causing the damage. After unrolling the painting on the work surface, proceed thus:

Step 1 Place your long plastic rule along the horizon or some other level feature, and holding it firmly in

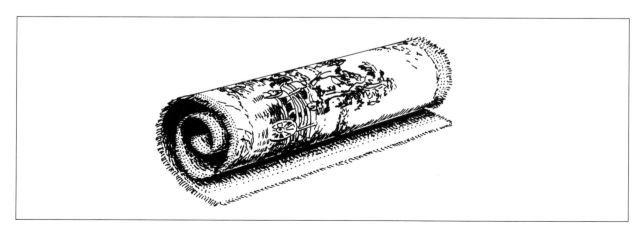

Correct way to roll unstretched oil painting for transit: artwork side faces outwards.

Squaring up an unstretched oil painting for framing.

place, position your square at the edge of the painting and lightly draw a line at 90° to the horizon.

Step 2   Repeat this at the other edge of the painting, though before moving the rule, draw a line ½in (12mm) long at the very edges of the canvas, to mark the horizon. You now have two lines at 90° to the horizon which should be extended right along the sides of the canvas.

STRETCHERS
A set of traditional artist's canvas stretchers of appropriate size can be purchased. These are available in various lengths. To assemble, slot them together at each corner; wedges are then inserted on the inner side so the frame can be expanded by tapping the wedges and so putting slight tension on the canvas after fixing. Some stretchers have a front and a back; the front edge is the chamfered one.

Step 3   From the horizon or level marks, measure both upwards and downwards and mark the position of the corners; this will determine the size of stretcher frame needed.

Step 4   Assemble the stretcher frame: slot the corners together, making sure they are square and tightly closed, but do not yet insert the wedges. Place the canvas face down on your protected surface and locate the stretcher over the pencilled outline; an easy guide is to push pins through from the front at each corner.

Step 5   Then bring the canvas round and fix a tack or staple in the centre of each side; after checking that the painting is level – that is, that the horizon is not running downhill or any buildings are leaning – tack to within 3in (75mm) of each corner. I like to make my corner folds by bringing the corner of the canvas over in line with the join of the stretcher, then folding each side over to make a 45° line over the join; I then tack in place. Repeat for each corner.

Step 6   When the corners are complete, insert the eight wedges and lightly tension the canvas.

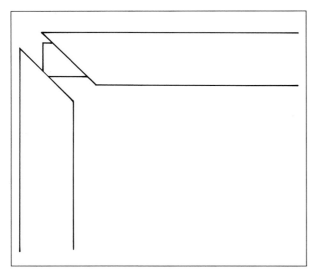

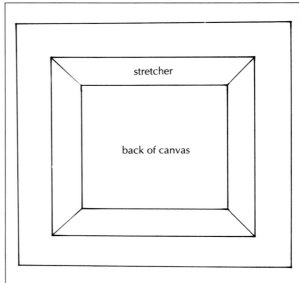

(a) Corner of oil painting stretcher. (b) With the painting face down, place stretcher centrally over the canvas. (c) Starting from the centre of each side, tack the edges of the canvas to the stretcher.

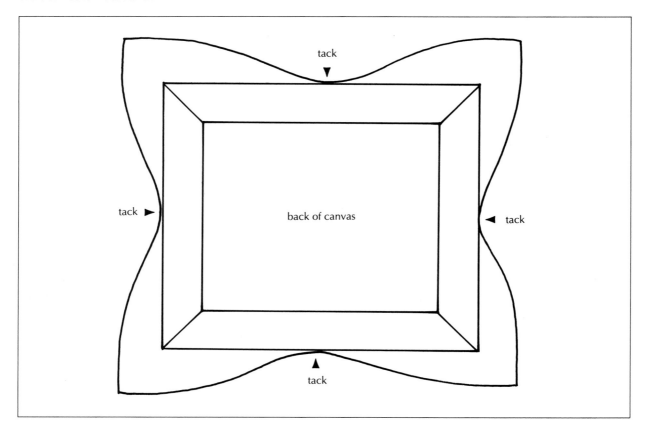

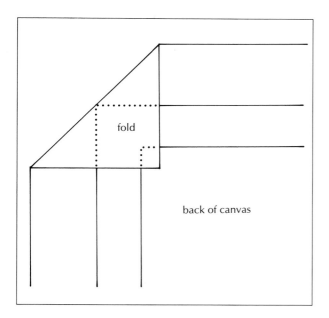

Forming the hospital corners. (This must be done before the wedges are inserted.) The first fold.

The corner: second fold.

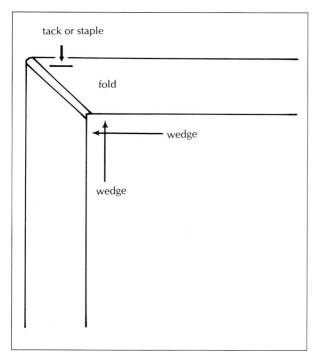

The corner: third fold.

8

Framing Pieces with Depth

DÉCOUPAGE

Artwork with depth such as découpage must be put in a deep box frame so it avoids any contact with the glass. This is achieved by putting a frame within a frame. The first consideration is the overall size of the artwork and any mount colour, then the depth needed to clear the glass. Decisions must also be made regarding the profile and finish of the inner frame, whether to use a moulding with an angled or a straight side, and if the finish is to be plain polished, stained, or painted to match the outer frame. In the example shown I have decided to use a straight moulding finished with a coat of wax polish. The procedure for construction is as follows:

Step 1 Apply polish to the length of moulding, and buff it to a semi-gloss; then mitre and joint as described in the chapter on frame making.

Step 2 Take the external measurements of this frame, and make the outer frame so the inner one is a snug fit.

Step 3 Now cut, clean and fit the glass, and fix the inner frame in place either by gluing or wedging as illustrated.

Step 4 One final check that the glass is perfectly clean and that there are no loose pieces of dust, and we are ready to fit the artwork. This should have the mount attached, either with glue or double-sided tape.

Step 5 Place the artwork in the inner frame and fix with small pins or glazer's points. The back can now be finished by taping to seal against dust; this technique is fully described in the final chapter.

Measuring the depth of découpage.

Here the box moulding is being tried over the découpage to check the fit.

Make the inner box frame a snug fit, and after fitting the glass run adhesive along the joints and allow it to set overnight.

The completed frame ready for sealing.

The frame, glass, board with aperture and velvet with the tools needed to mount the medal.

MEDALS

Medals can be framed either in a double frame or by spacing the mount away from the glass with strips of balsa wood. I like to cover the mount board with a piece of velvet; it is worth visiting your local fabric shop, as these establishments often have remnants which can be purchased at a reasonable cost.

Step 1 Decide on the overall size of the mount, then place the medal on it and draw round it with a pencil; this can be cut out by hand using a scalpel.
Step 2 Cover the mount with velvet; to make a neat job of the aperture, use the techniques described in the chapter on mount decoration. Place the mount face up on a flat surface, and press in the medal which will fit tightly.
Step 3 Make the frame as normal. After fitting the glass, cut four pieces of strip balsa wood; these can be tinted to match the moulding. Glue these into the re-

The mount has been covered with the velvet and the medal inserted into the aperture.

Balsa wood spacers fitted in the frame ready to accept the mounted medal.

The completed frame.

bate, taking care that no glue finds its way onto the glass.

The mount with the medal attached and the backing board can now be fitted, and the back finished off.

PASTELS

Special care is needed when handling and framing pastels: it is absolutely essential that they have no contact with the glass, as the image will quickly transfer from the paper to the glass. A hinged mount is the simple solution. Great care must also be taken when handling them, as they are easily smudged if they have not been fixed. If the artist wants you to fix the drawing, only use specially made fixative which will not harm or discolour; follow the manufacturer's instructions regarding application, and make sure there is adequate ventilation.

ETCHINGS

Etchings, particularly if they are limited editions, are best protected by placing them in a hinged mount made of conservation board. It is important to show any signature and edition number, and it is also usual to show any plate mark (the indentation produced around the picture when the etched plate is printed on the paper). The paper used is often top quality watercolour paper, of Not finish; some artists use handmade paper and have it watermarked with their name.

This type of artwork can inspire creative ideas from the framer, both in choice of mount colour and shape. For example I have some etchings with shaped tops and rounded corners, and I decided to follow this outline. So as to cut the mount as accurately as possible, I first traced the outline onto good quality tracing paper; then, using a flexible curve, I extended these measurements the required distance from the plate mark, namely two widths of the flexible curve. The next oper-

Tracing the outline of the arch top in preparation for cutting a matching shaped mount.

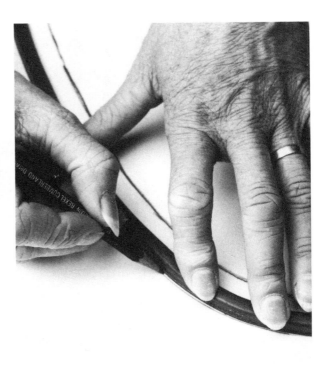

Two widths of the flexible curve was decided on as the appropriate distance between the mount and the etching. This is marked on the tracing paper.

After transferring the shape from the tracing paper to a sheet of board the aperture is cut out to give a template which can be used again. (If it is unlikely that more mounts of this shape will be cut the template stage can be omitted and the outline transferred straight to the conservation board.)

Guide the cutter around the curves with forward pressure being applied by the thumb of the left hand and the right hand controlling direction.

A selection of arch top mounts cut using the techniques described. (Reproduced by kind permission of Graham Clarke.)

ation was to cut around this mark carefully with a scalpel to make a template, which was then taped to the back of a sheet of conservation mount board large enough to contain the complete etching (trimming the paper will reduce the value of the work, so should not be contemplated). A pencil line was then drawn around the inner edge of the template, and this was very carefully cut using the Logan hand cutter and a straight-edge.

TIP

When following curves I find the easiest method is to guide the cutter with my right hand, keeping light forward pressure on with the left hand, and moving very slowly. It is a time-consuming process, but the end product is worth the care and effort.

9

Final Assembly and Finishing

We will now turn our attention to the back of the frame. Assuming that the glass has been polished and fitted, and the mount and artwork put into place, we must now consider the backing board; plywood, hardboard and framer's grey board are the materials used most. The backing board should be cut the same size as the glass; when plywood and hardboard are used, an acid-free barrier board must be positioned between the artwork and the board to prevent the transfer of any contamination from the ply or hardboard to the artwork. This barrier is not necessary when using framer's grey board which is cut to size with a sharp knife or guillotine. Plywood is cut using a fine-toothed saw and the cut edges must be smoothed with either a plane or sandpaper. Hardboard

can be cut using either a saw or a sharp Stanley knife and finished as for plywood.

When the backing board is flush with the moulding proceed as follows:

Step 1 Plane the edge to create a bevel; this will allow the pins or glazer's points to be angled into the moulding.

Step 2 Alternatively, insert extra mount board, bringing the backing level flush with, or slightly proud of, the moulding back; let the backing board overlap, allowing you to staple through the board and into the moulding. Fixings should be placed 1in (25mm) either side of the corners and at approximately 3in (75mm) intervals.

Here the bevel has been planed to allow the points to be fired in at an angle. Pins could be tapped in just as easily.

Here packing pieces have been placed alongside the artwork to give an even base for the backing board to sit on.

The backing board is in place and is stapled to the moulding ready to be taped.

SEALING THE BACK

Using Tape

The next step is to seal the back using 2in (50mm) brown gummed tape, the adhesive of which is activated by moistening; use a sponge standing in a saucer of water for this purpose.

When the backing board is below the back edge of the moulding proceed thus:

Step 1   Roughly measure the length needed to tape one long side, then place the tape adhesive side up and wipe it over with the sponge; leave it a few seconds for the adhesive to activate, then position it approximately ¼in (6mm) from the outer edge of the moulding.

Step 2   Stretching it tightly, press it onto the moulding, keeping it clear of the backing board. Then take the scalpel and cut the tape at both corners, flush with the shorter sides of the frame.

Step 3   Now, run your finger along the edge of the

When the tape has been moistened, stretch it along the edge of the moulding. Try to keep it clear of the backing sheet at this stage.

The next step is to cut the tape close to the corner, stopping when you reach the moulding.

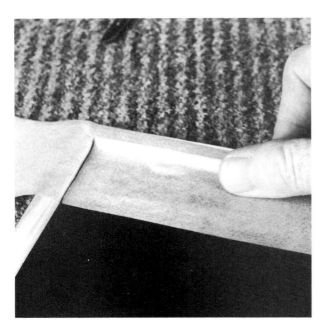

After cutting the tape at each side, gently press it into the corner, smoothing it out as you go. Repeat in each corner.

When the backing board overlaps the moulding, stretch the tape across the board so it is level with the moulding when viewed from above.

moulding, pressing the tape to give a tight turn; and with the tip of your finger, press it into the corner where the backing board meets the moulding.

Step 4   Smooth the tape onto the backing board, making sure there are no wrinkles; trim off the excess tape so there is an even space between tape and moulding edge all the way round.

Step 5   Repeat this on the other three sides, and you should have a neatly finished and sealed frame.

When the backing board overlaps the moulding edge proceed as follows:

Step 1   First place the adhesive tape onto the backing board in a position where the free edge lines up with the edge of the moulding.

Step 2   Smooth it down on the backing board, and run your finger on the edge of the backing pressing it into the corner where it meets the moulding; this brings the free edge in, so it does not overlap the outer edge of the moulding.

Step 3   The corners are finished as you go, by cutting the tape with the scalpel close to the backing board and smoothing it down onto the moulding. Trim off the

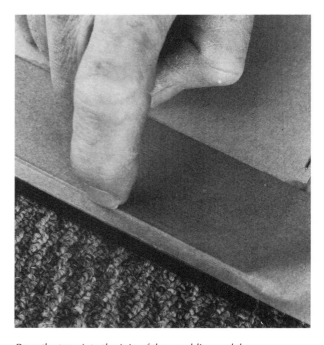

Press the tape into the join of the moulding and the board, then trim the corners.

excess to give an equal gap on all sides between tape edge and moulding edge.

Using Turn Buttons

When finishing a frame which needs to be opened at intervals it is pointless to tape and seal the back, and this is where turn buttons are used. Made from plastic, they are inserted into holes drilled in the back of the moulding, and can be turned to hold the back in place, or turned again to allow access to the contents of the frame. They are usually spaced as normal backing fixings.

STANDING FRAMES

Frames can be made to stand, though usually they are no larger than 10 × 8in (254 × 200mm) as stability otherwise becomes a problem. In fact the only difference in a standing frame is the back board which must be made from hardboard, as cardboard is not strong enough; a leg is attached to this by means of a bar and hinge. Construct this as follows:

Step 1 Measure from the top of the back to a third of the way down, and place the bar centrally; mark the two holes with your pencil.

Step 2 Remove the back and place it on a piece of scrap wood, and then drill out the two holes, cleaning any swarf from the underside.

Step 3 Place a bifurcated rivet through the bar and back, then turn the back over and with the rivet head resting on a hard surface, insert a screwdriver in the rivet and bend the legs outwards; finish off by hammering them flat. Repeat this operation on the second hole in the bar.

Drilling a ⅛in (3mm) hole prior to fitting the turn button. Note the tape around the drill shank – this is my depth gauge to prevent drilling too deep which would spoil the moulding.

Gently tap the turn button until it lies flush with the moulding.

This is a strut back. It is fitted to the frame in place of the backing board when the picture (usually a photograph) is to stand.

At the top is the hinge; note how the bifurcated rivets are fitted. At the bottom is the bar.

Use a screwdriver to spread the ends of the rivet, then flatten with a hammer on a hard surface to secure.

Step 4 To make the strut, measure from the bar to the base of the frame and cut a piece of hardboard to this length. In width this piece needs to be shaped so that the top is 2in (50mm) then widening to 3in (75mm) at the base.

Step 5 Following the drilling and riveting procedure, attach the hinge ¼in (6mm) below the top of the strut. After fitting the back in the frame and sealing with gummed paper, clip the hinge to the bar – and we now have a frame which will stand.

HANGING FRAMES

Most frames are intended to be hung on a wall and therefore need cord or wire attached to the back, and screw eyes of various sizes are used for this purpose.

Screw Eyes

These are available in three sizes: the smallest is 14 × 1, medium is 16 × 1, and large is 25 × 4. Small frames up to 10 × 8in (254 × 200mm) need a size 14 × 1; medium frames up to 16 × 20in (400 × 500mm) need the 16 × 1; and for anything over this size use the 25 × 4. If you are in any doubt as to which screw eye to use, choose the larger one to be sure the weight of the picture will not pull the screw eye open. If the frame is very weighty use a D-ring: this is screwed into the frame and is capable of supporting greater weights.

An alternative to screw eyes are **screw rings**: these are screw eyes with a ring attached; when the cord is

D-rings and screws, used when supporting a heavy frame.

threaded through the ring it lies away from the edge of the frame and is therefore less visible.

Always drill the holes for the screw eyes angling towards the top of the frame, and approximately ¼in (6mm) deep. This prevents the moulding splitting when the screw eye is inserted, and the upwards angle provides a stronger attachment than a screw eye inserted at 90°.

Alternatives

There are two alternatives to screw eyes and picture cord for lightweight frames – plastic D-rings and one-hole triangle hangers. These are attached to the back-board with a bifurcated rivet, and must be placed centrally or the frame will not hang straight.

A selection of screw eyes and screw rings.

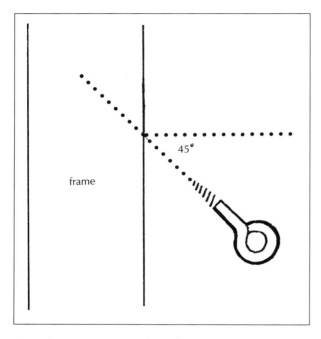

Fixing the screw eye. (Note the angle.)

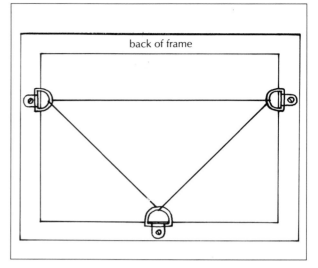

Supporting the bottom bar of a large frame to take the stress off the bottom joints.

Picture Cord

Picture cord is sized in numbers, starting with No 1 which has a breaking strain of 196lb (89kg), up to No 5 with a breaking strain of 742lb (337kg); the picture should be no heavier than half of the breaking strain. When tying the cord, put as much tension on it as you can without bending the screw eye; use a reef knot, and then tie an extra knot to secure it and prevent it slipping or working loose.

HANGING YOUR PICTURES

Choose how and where you hang your pictures carefully:

● Try to avoid direct sunlight as this will spoil the artwork or photograph.
● Hang your pictures in groups, with a large picture forming a base, and balanced with several smaller pictures.
● A large picture will hang better if two picture hooks

EXTRA SUPPORT

Some frames need the bottom bar supporting because the weight of the glass will put undue stress on the lower joints. This extra support is achieved by fitting a D-ring in the centre of the lower bar, and threading the picture cord or wire through this and the two side supports.

---

are used; it will be far more stable and you will not have to keep straightening it up.
● If pictures are hung on a cold wall or directly above a radiator it is advisable to attach small spacers to the bottom rail of the frame; this will allow air to circulate behind the picture thus reducing the possibility of damp and mould damage.

TIP

Pictures can also be hung using picture wire. This is not as strong as cord, but it will give your framing a more up-market appearance. Choose wire capable of carrying twice the picture weight. Use ferrules to anchor the wire, and secure it by crimping with pliers or a purpose-made crimping tool. Take care when using wire, as stray strands are liable to prick your finger.

Index

Numbers in italics indicate illustrations.

acid 49
adhesives 23
artwork
  cropping *53*
  deep pieces 110, 114, *114–19*, 116–17, 119
  mounting 67–8, *67–9*
  squaring up 55, *55*
  valuable 14, 50, 67, 68
assembly area of workshop 10

backing *see* finishing
backing boards 120, *120–1*
box frames, deep *see* artwork: deep pieces

carpenter's vice 9, *11*
certificates 90
conservation quality mount board 49–50
corner clamping vice 10, *11*, *25*
cutting mats 12, *12*

decoration of mounts *see* mount decoration
découpage 114, *114–15*

electricity supply 14
embroideries *see* needlework
etchings 117, *118–19*, 119

fillers, wood 33
finishing
  backing boards 120, *120*
  sealing the back 121–3, *121–3*
  turn buttons 123, *123*
finishing area of workshop 12, *13*
Fontenay Base 99–100, *99*
frame components *17*

gesso 101, *101–2*
gilding 12, 99–101, *99–102*
glass
  calculating size 38
  cleaning 44, *44–5*
  measuring *38*
  quality 35
glass cutters 12, *12*, 35, *35*
glass-cutting 34, *37*, 38, *39*, 40, *40–1*
  plastic glass 42, *42–3*
glass-cutting area of workshop 12
glue 23

hanging frames 125, *125–6*
hanging pictures 126
heating 14
Hogarth moulding 90, *90*

Ingrès board 46, *47*

jointing 14, *14*, 15, *15*, 23, *24–9*, 25, 27, *31–3*, 32–3

left-hand mitres 18, 19, *21*
lighting 14

maps 90
medals 116–17, *116–17*
mitre blocks 18, *18*, 19, *20*, *21*, 22
mitre cutting 15, *15*, 17–18, *19–23*, 21–2, *24*, 27, 31, *31*
mitring area of workshop 10
modern prints 90
mouldings
  calculating length 30, *30*
  choosing *17*, 30, *30*, 88, *88–90*, 90
  finishes 92, *93*, *96*
  gesso 101, *101–2*
  gilding 99–100
  making 91–2, *92–8*, 94, 96, 97
  samples *17*, 18, *18*
  storage 16, *16*, 18, *18*
mount boards
  calculating size *51*, *52*, 54, *54*
  colour 50
  double mounts 53, *53*, *55*
  identifying 46, *47*
  marking out 56, *56*
  museum quality 50
  neutral pH 49
  production 48–9
  proportions 51, *51*
  size and quality 48, *48*, *49*
  types 49–50
mount cutters 46, 56, 58, 62, *62*
mount cutting 46, 57–8, *57–66*, 61–3, 66
  etchings 117–19, *118*, *119*
mount decoration
  cutting out motifs 79, *79*
  deckled edge 87, *87*
  decorative material 83, *83*
  decorative paper 80, *80–2*, 81–2

embossing 84, *84–6*
lining 70, *70–8*, 72, 74, 76, 78
mounting artwork 67–8, *67–9*
    deep pieces 110, 114, *114–19*, 116–17, 119
    see also needlework

needlework 14
    quilting 110, *110*
    small pieces 109, *109*
    stretching 103–8, *103–8*

oil paintings 110–11, *110–13*

pastels 117
picture cord 126
plastic glass 42, *42–3*
polishing 92, *93*
power supply 14

quilting 110, *110*

right-hand mitres *20*, 21–2

samplers *see* needlework
saws: mitre 15, 18, *18*

screw eyes 125, *125–6*
sealing the back 121–3, *121–3*
self-adhesive tape: for lining 78, *78*
sizing 49
staining 92, *93*
standing frames 123, 124, *124*

T-Square 36, *36*, *37*, *39*
tapestries *see* needlework
tools
    essential 14–15, *14*
    glass-cutting 34, *34*
    moulding 91, *91*
    mount curtting 46, *56*, *58*, 62, *62*
traditional prints 90
turn buttons 123, *123*

vices 9, 10, *11*, *25*

watercolours 88, 90
wood fillers 33
woodpulp 49
woodworking vice 9, 11
work surface 9, *9*
workshop layout 9–10, *9*, *10*, *11*, 12, *13*